Briti

7

002

19

13

003

4

3 0 SEP 2009

0 9 FEB 2009

1 1 JAN 2008

British Prisons

Second Edition

MIKE FITZGERALD and JOE SIM

Basil Blackwell · Oxford

© Mike Fitzgerald and Joe Sim 1979, 1982

First edition 1979
Second edition first published 1982

Basil Blackwell, Publisher Limited
108 Cowley Road, Oxford OX4 1JF, England

British Library Cataloguing in Publication Data

Fitzgerald, Mike
   British prisons.—2nd ed.
   I. Title   II. Sim, Joe
   365′.941   HV 9647
ISBN 0 631 12529 9
ISBN 0 631 12606 6 Pbk

Typesetting by David Green Printers Limited
Kettering Northamptonshire
Printed in Great Britain

Contents

Preface to the Second Edition

This is the third version of *British Prisons*, first published in May 1979. The book has been extensively revised and updated to take account of recent developments in the prison system. It aims to provide a critical introduction to British prisons, examining the nature and extent of imprisonment, types of prison, the situation of prisoners, and particular issues and controversies in the adult prison system. We have not included information on young offenders.

A special feature of the book is that information on prisons in both England and Wales, and in Scotland is included. The prison systems in these countries are historically and organizationally separate, and we have sought to compare and contrast their different penal policies and practices. Unless explicitly identified, the text refers to both systems.

As with anyone wanting to find out about prisons, we have been hampered by the obsessive secrecy of the prison departments. Access to, and information about British prisons is controlled and selective, and so we have supplemented official pronouncements with information from prisoners and ex-prisoners, prison staff, criminologists, media reports and people active in the struggle for penal change.

To all the people who helped us prepare the book we extend our thanks. It has been a long and difficult process, beset by libel actions, which dragged on for over a year and led to the withdrawal of the original version and the the cancellation of a revised one. The present revision, completed in January 1981, has similarly been delayed for extensive checking. Throughout it all, the publishers, Basil Blackwell, have been tremendously supportive, and we are very grateful to them.

Particular thanks are due also to Gill Blowers, Geoff Coggan of the National Prisoners Movement (PROP), Pat Craddock, Paul Fitzgerald, Dave Godwin of the Scottish Council for Civil Liberties, Paul Gordon, Victoria Greenwood, Stuart Hall, Meg Howarth, Frank Keeley, Michelle Kent, Carol Johns, Greg McLennan, Dave McDonald, John Muncie and Phil Scraton.

Finally, this book is the result of a genuinely co-operative effort. We sat down and wrote every word together. Any mistakes are our responsibility, but we have tried to write as accurate an account of the British prison system as our understanding and the present restrictions on information allow.

The ultimate expression of law is not order – it's prison. We have hundreds upon hundreds of prisons, and thousands upon thousands of laws, yet there is no social order, no social peace.

George Jackson, 1972

One sign of success in the fight for law and order is that more people are in prison.

Merlyn Rees, Home Secretary, 1978

1 CRISIS IN BRITISH PRISONS

At the beginning of November 1978, Merlyn Rees, then the British Home Secretary, announced the setting up of an urgent, independent inquiry into the prison system of the United Kingdom. The inquiry, Mr Rees told the House of Commons, would examine the organization and management of the prison system, including its use of resources and working arrangements, conditions in prison service establishments, and the structure, pay and conditions of the staff. The Home Secretary's action was welcomed by Parliament, the prison governors, prison officers and prison reform groups, although not without reservations.

Why had the inquiry been set up? Less than a year previously, the Home Office had published *Prisons and the Prisoner*, which, it was said, provided an up-to-date, informative and authoritative account of penal policy and practice in England and Wales.[1] Mr Rees himself, in a Foreword, had introduced the booklet as 'an attempt to respond to a situation where widespread anxiety about serious crime and delinquency is matched by increasing concern about the measures needed to care for and control those committed to custody by the courts'.[2]

Prisons and the Prisoner was published to supersede its predecessor, *People in Prison*,[3] produced in 1969. The anonymous authors of the new booklet were aware that events in the prisons might make at least part of it redundant rather quickly. And the *Report of the Work of the Prison Department in England and Wales*

---

[1] *Prisons and the Prisoner*, 1977.
[2] ibid., Foreword.
[3] *People in Prison*, 1969.

for 1977 made it abundantly clear that the 'authoritative statement of the policy and practice' of the penal service had failed to take sufficient account of the 'severe practical problems' facing the service.[4] These 'severe practical problems' finally provoked the government into setting up the inquiry that was designed to provide a temporary breathing space and prevent the prison system falling headlong into chaos. For what everyone did agree about was that at the end of 1978 the prison system was in crisis.

In the weeks prior to Mr Rees's announcement, the media had brought the problems of the prison system sharply into focus. The daily prison population (including young offenders) hovered around 42,000 in England and Wales, and 5,000 in Scotland. Conditions inside were generally appalling, and allegations of serious malpractice were being levelled against prison staff and the prison authorities. In particular, the use of drugs to control prisoners was being widely publicised, despite, or perhaps because of, denials by the Home Office. Prisoners had become more vociferous and organized in their protests against inhumane and intolerable conditions. In court at Hull, prison officers and an assistant prison governor faced charges of assaulting and beating prisoners in the aftermath of the riot at Hull gaol in August 1976. A former prison officer had testified that he and colleagues had beaten up prisoners while other officers stood by. Prison governors warned of the immediate and total breakdown of the prison system and complained loudly of the 'deplorable lack of leadership' from the Home Office.[5] Prison officers were engaged in an increasingly militant campaign of disruption of the prisons, against the orders of their union, the Prison Officers' Association (POA). At Parkhurst, prison officers refused to take in any more prisoners; at Brixton, they refused to accept defendants remanded by the courts; at Wandsworth, workshops closed and outside contract work was refused. Disruptive action was threatened at forty of Britain's 120 penal establishments, including a ban on overtime, severe restrictions on prison visits, recreation and association, and refusal either to escort prisoners to, or receive them from the courts. In Scotland, prison officers threatened widespread

[4]*Report of the Work of the Prison Department in England and Wales,* 1977: Paragraph 1.
[5]*The Times,* 30 October 1978.

and crippling industrial action when the decision not to reopen the notorious segregation unit (known as the 'cages') at Inverness prison was taken by the Secretary of State for Scotland.

It was in an effort to defuse this grave and rapidly deteriorating situation that the inquiry was set up. In particular, it was in response to the prison officers' demands for improved pay and conditions, which had been the immediate cause of their disruptive activities. The depth of their sense of grievance was shown by the initial refusal of some branches of the POA to call off their industrial action despite the inquiry. Only when it was agreed (in writing) that the inquiry would cover pay and conditions of officers, did some officers in England and Wales suspend their actions, pending the published report. In Scotland, the unofficial work-to-rule went ahead, and about 2,000 prisoners in four Scottish prisons were immediately affected.

At the end of 1978, these were the most visible manifestations of the crisis in the prisons. The activities of the prison officers had led the prison governors to warn that there could be 'a serious loss of control which has to be quelled by armed intervention with the probability of both staff and prisoners being killed'.[6] Governors had repeatedly warned senior Home Office officials and junior Ministers of the gravity of the situation. Their warnings, not for the first time, had gone unheeded. For the crisis in the prisons so widely discussed in November 1978 was not new. Rather, the prison system in Britain has been in a perpetual state of crisis since the Gladstone Committee report of 1895. Peter Timms, governor at Maidstone prison, pointed out that there have been recurring prison crises, to which successive governments have generally sought some immediate palliative to submerge the problem, only for it to 'raise its head with an added sting at a later time'.[7] The pattern of crisis – partial inquiry – crisis – partial inquiry was being repeated yet again.

Since 1970, up to the setting up of the May Inquiry, there had been numerous reports in the media of crises in the prisons. Editorial after editorial, feature article after feature article referred habitually to 'the crisis in the prisons'. In 1970, Hugh Klare, Director of the Howard League for Penal Reform, insisted that the 'British penal

---

[6] *The Times*, 1 November 1978.
[7] *Community Care*, 15 November 1978, 20.

system is faced with a crisis.'[8] Later that year, *The Times* warned that 'prisons can no longer cope';[9] and the General Secretary of the Prison Officers' Association commented that the 'situation is critical and frightening. I do not use these words normally, and I am not trying to create a panic situation, but something will have to be done.'[10] In 1972, there were over a hundred massive, peaceful demonstrations by prisoners, and again the lead writers were busy. In 1973, the *Prison Officers' Magazine* headlined its December editorial: 'Crisis Point'.[11] In 1975, a *Prison Service Journal* editorial on the crisis, pointed out that if 'nothing is done to avert [the crisis] and the trend persists, the prison service in this country will be placed in a situation quite disgraceful by national and international standards.'[12]

In 1976, the disturbance at Hull had stimulated crisis headlines again, and *The Times* ran three special features headed the 'Crisis in prisons'. In 1977, references to 'crisis' were scattered throughout the year. In January, Nicholas Hinton, then Director of the National Association for the Care and Resettlement of Offenders, addressed a joint parliamentary penal affairs group on 'the prison crisis'.[13] In March, in a major House of Commons debate on the prisons, member after member spoke of 'the crisis inside'.[14]

In May 1978, *The Times* reported that the crisis in the prison system was 'a crisis of faith as well as money'.[15]

On 1 November 1978, a lead article in *The Times*, headlined 'High Risk Prisons', argued that the 'discontent of the prison officers . . . is only one symptom of a crisis facing the whole prison service.'[16] The previous day, the *Guardian* had described the 'volcano behind the bars'.[17]

Only after many 'crisis' years, had a partial enquiry into the prison

---

[8]*The Times*, 31 August 1970.
[9]ibid., 14 October 1970.
[10]*The Times*, 5 August 1970.
[11]*Prison Officers' Magazine*, December 1973.
[12]*Prison Service Journal*, June 1975.
[13]*The Times*, 29 January 1977.
[14]*Listener*, 3 March 1977.
[15]*The Times*, 29 January 1977.
[16]ibid. 1 November 1978.
[17]*Guardian*, 31 October 1978.

service been set up. That it would fall short of the much-needed review of penal policy and practice was feared by many, and with the publication of the Report, these fears proved well founded.

The Report, which eventually appeared in October 1979, was received with an overwhelming sense of disappointment, anger and betrayal. Within a year, the prison officers were engaged in massive industrial action, and refusing to allow new prisoners into prisons. Police cells were being used to house those refused entry to the prisons, and on 31 October 1980, the anniversary of the publication of the May Report, troops moved into Frankland, a new maximum security prison, opened, uncompleted, nine months ahead of schedule, to relieve the intense pressure on police cells. The Home Secretary assumed staggering new powers, under the Imprisonment (Temporary Powers) Act, which passed through Parliament in a day and a half. The Act was described by Larry Grant, chairperson of the National Council of Civil Liberties, as 'one of the most dangerous laws to be put on the statute book since the war'.[18]

The May Inquiry, which had an opportunity not simply to review but to break fundamentally with the 150-year-old pattern of more prisons and more prisoners, was forgotten. It had passed up this chance, preferring, like so many inquiries before it, to represent the recipe for prison crisis as a recipe for prison salvation. It simply hadn't worked.[19]

The May Inquiry proved a redundant exercise, not least because it failed to recognize the nature and full extent of the crisis in the British prison system. Indeed there is not one crisis, rather a whole series, which taken together account for the parlous state of the prisons. In this introductory chapter we want to begin to explore them. In particular, we will focus on the crisis of 'visibility', 'authority', 'conditions', 'containment', and finally 'legitimacy'. While we have separated these for the purpose of discussion, it is important to remember that they are interwoven in the complex web which is 'the crisis in British prisons'.

---

[18] *State Research Bulletin* No. 21, 33.
[19] For a detailed critique of the May Report see Fitzgerald and Sim, 1980.

VISIBILITY

Since the centralization of penal institutions in England and Wales and in Scotland in 1878, prisons have usually been as effective in shutting out the enquirer as they have in keeping in the prisoner. The Webbs pointed out:

> One of the unforseen results of the transfer of the local prisons to the administration of a Government Department was to put a stop to even the small amount of publicity that had since 1835 prevailed . . . The reports of the inspectors upon the administration of what had become their own Department were quickly found to be different from those made upon the administration of other authorities. Moreover, when the inspectors expressed themselves freely upon particular abuses, it was deemed inconvenient to make their strictures known to the public. Any reports of this character became confidential documents; and the Prison Commissioners presented to Parliament their own general reports, in which they described their own administration . . . But the inevitable bias of any official administration is to avoid the trouble that is caused by scandals, and even by the questions put in the House of Commons by members who had got hold of the particular abuses from which no administration can ever be entirely free. Nothing was therefore published that was likely to give rise to Parliamentary complaint, or afford a handle to newspaper criticism. The visits of non-official persons to the prisoners was severely discouraged.[20]

As the Webbs concluded, 'the prison became a "silent world", shrouded so far as the public is concerned in almost complete darkness.'[21]

The 1922 Amendment to the Official Secrets Act of 1911 dealt specifically with matters of internal state security, and has subsequently been applied to prison systems. The prison departments of England and Wales and Scotland have maintained a

---

[20]Webb and Webb, 1963, 216–17.
[21]ibid., 235.

near monopoly on information about what goes on inside the prison walls.

In their infrequent discussions of penal policy and practice, successive Home Secretaries have used the lack of public knowledge and scrutiny of prisons to support their particular needs. On the one hand they have argued for 'substantial popular interest and support for the aims of an enlightened penal policy and for the methods we use to carry it out.'[22] On the other hand, they have systematically denied the public access to information on, and debates about penal affairs. Uninformed and 'reactionary' public opinion is then claimed to be the barrier to the introduction of enlightened policies. In Britain, we still do not have the right to know what goes on in the prisons.

As Laurie Taylor has pointed out, if John Howard was working and writing today:

> The Home Office would have prevented him getting anywhere near such abuses, just as it has excluded independent psychiatrists, lawyers, and researchers, stifled parliamentary debate on prison policy, and muted prisoners' complaints. When Rees declares that 'the lot of prisoners is not a subject that normally arouses the interest of people in general', he is not, as he believes, simply recording an unfortunate and arbitrary feature of national consciousness, he is also describing the predictable results of years of Home Office secrecy and circumlocution.
>
> To talk of public lack of interest in prisons in such circumstances is tantamount to taking the populace to task for its lack of concern about the recent design of tactical nuclear warheads.[23]

The prison authorities have frequently misled and misinformed the public about prisons. To take one example: in six weeks in 1977, the Home Office managed to come up with no fewer than five conflicting explanations of three, new, windowless and sound-proofed cells at Brixton prison in London. Originally, it denied the

---

[22]*The Times*, 12 June 1974.
[23]Taylor, 1978, 172.

existence of the cells at all. The *Guardian* was later told that the cells did exist, and were for 'unmanageable prisoners'. At the same time, a reporter from the *Nursing Times* was informed by the Home Office that the cells were for epileptics, and this was confirmed by Mr Brynmor John, Home Office Minister of State. Further enquiries by the *Nursing Times* produced yet another contradictory explanation. Apparently the cells were part of a new library, not yet in use, and were temporarily housing the education officers. Two MPs then wrote to the Home Office asking for the confusion to be cleared up. Lord Harris, Minister with responsibility for prisons, replied that the cells were for use of solicitors wanting to interview Category A clients. A Home Office spokesman agreed that this was their purpose although they were not actually being used as interview rooms and eventually would form part of the new library. He added that the previous explanations were wrong because information had been given to newspaper enquiries which 'had not been very specific'.[24] The prison authorities' near monopoly of information about prison events has recently been challenged. In particular, the work of The National Prisoners' Movement (PROP), formed in 1972, has been a constant thorn in the side of the Home Office. That the media have been so ready to listen to PROP is a testimony to the frustration which many journalists must experience when researching and writing about prisons, and to the success of PROP in providing an alternative and reliable source of news about the prisons which has frequently been at odds with official versions of events. The events which followed a riot at Hull prison illustrate this.

Following a riot at Hull prison in 1976, PROP published detailed accounts of the aftermath of the rooftop protest which revealed that prisoners who had taken part in the disturbance were beaten and their personal property destroyed by some prison officers. Such allegations are frequently made, but rarely investigated. After the Parkhurst riot in 1969, for example, during which thirty-five officers and twenty-eight prisoners were injured, charges of brutality by prison staff were ignored. Indeed, one member of the prison service wrote, at the time:

In the past, far too much has been made of alleged brutality by

---

[24] *Guardian*, 10 February 1977.

prison staff. In fact, it would be fair to say that this does not exist outside the fantasies of former prisoners, looking for a gimmick with which to peddle their memories, or television commentators, trying to sell false social values. . . . In the last decade, only three prison officers have come to trial for using excessive force in restraining inmates, and all of them were acquitted.[25]

The Home Office was unable to conceal the events at Hull. Protests by PROP, MPs and others led to the setting up of a police investigation into prison officers' activities after the prisoners had come down from the rooftops. The original Home Office inquiry into the Hull riot completely exonerated prison staff, apart from remarking on the occasional 'excess of zeal' which particular officers had shown. But at the end of 1978, more than two years after the event, eight prison officers were found guilty of charges arising out of the aftermath of the prisoners' demonstration. The officers were charged with conspiring together and with others to assault and beat prisoners. At the committal proceedings, Major Peter Lionel James of the Home Office had told the court of an orgy of destruction by prison officers after the riot. He described the prison officers as 'a mob trying to control a mob', and acknowledged that prisoners' property had been destroyed; photographs of wives and families had been torn up; transistors and gramophone records had been destroyed; and caged birds belonging to prisoners had been killed.[26]

The attack on prison secrecy has gathered momentum not only as outsiders decry the lack of visibility of the prisons, but as prison staff increasingly complain of having to remain silent, on a penalty of imprisonment under the Official Secrets Act. As two assistant governors have written, of necessity, anonymously:

It is sometimes forgotten that we are concerned with the lives of people in custody and not with state secrets. Probation officers, social workers and hospital administrators, whose work, in many respects, is similar to that of prison officials, are regulated by 'professional integrity and judgement' in their dealings

---

[25]*Prison Officers' Magazine,* December 1969.
[26]*Guardian,* 2 November 1978; *The Times,* 2 November 1978.

with the public and are not required to sign the Official Secrets Act.

This all-pervasive Act not only inhibits disclosures of injustices which inevitably occur in any system but also prevents open dialogue between those within and outside the prison service wishing to improve the quality of training in our prisons and borstals. The ruling that prison officials should not express a view publicly leads to frustration, sterility and inertia.

Many of us working in the field feel we have something of value to contribute and would like to be encouraged to lend our practical experience and expertise to the debate on penal reform.[27]

The impact of secrecy is felt in every aspect of day-to-day life in individual establishments. Prisoners and prison officers have no right of access to many of the regulations, Standing Orders and Circular Instructions which they are supposed either to abide by or to enforce. Even governors, responsible for the running of individual establishments, can be denied information which has a direct bearing on their job.

The consequences of such secrecy can be disastrous.

In 1969, for example, prisoners at Parkhurst sent out a secret letter to the press, alleging brutality by prison officers. The Home Secretary, James Callaghan, ordered an urgent inquiry into the allegations, headed by Assistant Prison Director, Michael Gale. His report, which, according to the *Sunday Times* of 2 August 1970, acknowledged that the allegations were well founded, was with the Home Secretary in June. But few changes were made to the prison regime, and no charges were brought against prison officers. In October, Parkhurst erupted into the worst disturbance in British prisons since the 1932 Dartmoor Mutiny. The Gale Report has never been made public, and was never even seen by the governor of Parkhurst, who has since written: 'I was never allowed to see this report, as it was confidential, although I feel that it had a direct bearing on my future in the Service.'[28]

The recent disruption of the prison system has served to intensify

---

[27]Cited in Briggs, 1975, 22.
[28]Miller, 1976, 134.

the crisis of visibility. Slowly, but surely, the secrecy behind the prison walls is being breached, as alternative sources of information about the prisons are more securely established.

AUTHORITY

Since 1972, prison officers have been waging an increasingly disruptive and militant campaign within the prisons. In that year the prison system was rocked by what the Secretary of the POA called the 'most serious challenge to established control, good order and security that the Prison Service has had to endure in its history.'[29] Uniformed staff have been alarmed by recent developments in penal policy, which they see as undermining their authority within the prisons. In seeking to re-establish this authority, prison officers have conflicted with prisoners, governors, prison department officials, outsiders brought in to perform specialist tasks within the prison system, and even their own union, the Prison Officers' Association.

Conflict with the prisoner is perhaps the most obvious aspect of the officers' crisis of authority. Individually and collectively, staff have complained long and hard about what they see as the overriding concern for prisoners at the expense of uniformed staff. Letters published in the *Prison Officers' Magazine* reflect the bitterness felt by uniformed staff:

> I have been in the Service for some thirteen years and I have seen the pendulum gradually swing round in the inmates favour. . . .[30]

> For far too long everyone has been made aware of the criminals so called 'rights' but it is time that the rights and protection of the prison officer be brought to the fore.[31]

Attempts by prisoners to enforce the rule of law in prisons has heightened uniformed staff's anxieties:

[29]*Prison Officers' Magazine*, July 1973.
[30]*Prison Officers' Magazine*, April 1976.
[31]ibid.

It was with mixed feelings of anger and incredulity to [*sic*] read of colleagues at Cardiff being found guilty of alleged violence against inmates and even more that they were sentenced to terms of suspended imprisonment.[32]

Such feelings are clearly shared by the Chairman of the POA, who concluded his address to the 1977 annual conference with the warning that, 'the Prison Officers' Association will resist any attempt [by prisoners] to use the due processes of law and the administration of justice as means by which to attack our members.'[33]

Uniformed staff are particularly hostile towards prison reformers, criminologists and other outside commentators on penal affairs, whose influence is seen as contributing to prison officers' loss of authority:

Let's face it, the situation is deteriorating week by week, the corruption of our standards by so-called socially high-minded elements in our society (do-gooders to use the normal description) has begun to show itself in recent times. We cannot really blame prisoners for grasping the opportunities to show their utter contempt and disregard for our own authority. We can blame ourselves for allowing the do-gooder element to gain a substantial foothold in our Service – and well-entrenched they are, make no mistake about that. The day may come when the do-gooder element can no longer be tolerated and strong action will be needed to rid ourselves of them.[34]

Another officer, writing about the decision to suspend the use of the notorious control units in England and Wales, defined do-gooders as 'that misguided bunch of mental misfits whose main pleasure in life is riding on the proverbial bandwagon of public attention.'[35]

Prison officers' militancy has also reflected their uncertainty about the nature of their role in the prison system. Are uniformed staff

---

[32]ibid.

[33]*Prop*, Volume 2, Number 6, Winter 1978/9.

[34]*Prison Officers' Magazine*, December 1976.

[35]ibid., November 1976.

'gaolers' with an unambiguous custodial role, or are they 'welfare workers', with an involvement in treatment and training of prisoners? This question has been debated in a long-running 'saga' in the *Prison Officers' Magazine*:

> Over the past few years I have felt that the status of the prison officer has been gradually undermined, in spite of all the nonsense I have read from time to time about raising it . . . The prison officer of today is to my mind nothing more than 'a waiter' or a 'message boy' to his charges.[36]

Since 1963, the POA has been committed to securing a role for prison officers in the rehabilitation of offenders. At its annual conference that year the Association unanimously adopted the resolution:

> This Conference, being gravely aware of the dangerous trend in criminal behaviour within society today, agrees that the Association should endeavour to define what should be the modern role of the Prison Officer in connection with the rehabilitation of the prisoner. It further agrees that in order to enable the Prison Officer to take his full share in this responsible task he be trained to (a) assist and advise during the course of the sentence and (b) assist in after-care following an inmate's release insofar as this may prove practicable.[37]

But the day to day work of most prison officers remains routine, boring, repetitive and not far removed from the work of the turnkey in the nineteenth century. We shall explore this conflict of role at length in chapter 5. For the moment, it is important to recognize that the POA's inability to implement the 1963 conference resolution has been a critical factor in the crisis of authority experienced by many prison officers. The growing numbers of better paid, higher status, welfare professionals in prisons has served as a constant reminder to uniformed staff of their own inferior position. In their recent

---

[36]ibid., July 1972.
[37]*Prison Officers' Magazine*, November 1963.

industrial action, prison officers have shown their dissatisfaction with the influx of welfare workers, civilian instructors, teachers and other outsiders by denying them access to the prisons.

The crisis of authority has also been revealed in the worsening relationships between prison officers, and governors and prison department officials. The industrial unrest of the past eight years has severely strained already difficult working relationships. It has become increasingly clear that prison officers and governor grades compete for control of individual penal institutions. In 1975, for example, prison officers at Winchester unanimously passed a vote of no confidence in the governor, and demanded that he should be replaced. They complained he was 'too soft' with prisoners, and that discipline had declined.[38] A week later, after a four-hour meeting with officials of the Prison Officers' Association, the governor and the prison officers signed a nine-point plan designed to restore good working relations.[39]

Prison governors, in their evidence to the House of Commons Expenditure Committee, argued that prison staff now probably present more difficulties for them than prisoners.[40] Certainly, the prison departments would have to agree with that view. During the past eight years there has been industrial unrest and disruption by prison officers on a scale hitherto unimagined. Much of the dispute has centred on pay, and the extremely complex system of bonuses, overtime, and special allowances which prison officers recieve on top of their basic rates. Cuts in public expenditure have not only affected part of the prison building programme, but also limited the amount of overtime to be worked in any single institution. Prison officials have an ambiguous attitude towards overtime. They complain of working long hours, but have also taken industrial action to protest against cutbacks in these.

Relations with the central prison department have been at their worst since the early 1960s. As early as April 1961 an article in the *Prison Officers' Magazine* had claimed that morale was at 'a low ebb'.[41] The prison departments in England and Wales and Scotland

---

[38]*The Times*, 31 March 1975.
[39]*The Times*, 5 April 1975.
[40]ibid., 7 December 1978.
[41]Cited in Thomas, 1972, 195.

were reorganized in 1963, but soon appeared to prison officers as remote, 'grossly over-centralized and consequently inefficient', and as a place where 'matters of mainly human interest' were dealt with 'by people who are predominantly concerned with administrative matters'.[42]

In 1977, the Chairman of the Dartmoor Branch of the POA accused the Home Office of being 'completely out of touch with what happens in individual prisons',[43] and the annual conference condemned the prison department for using prison officers in a game of political chess.[44] In the aftermath of the major disturbance at Gartree prison in October 1978, officers at the prison have claimed:

> It has now become obvious, even to the general public, that these misguided people in the Home Office responsible for the administration of the Prison Service have failed dismally. The Home Office Prison Department can now be seen for what it really is - a rambling, inefficient, bureaucratic machine that seems unable to correct itself despite being constantly reminded of its inadequacy.[45]

Predictably, it is prisoners who have borne the brunt of prison officers' disruptive action, which has resulted in extra restrictions on visits, association, recreation and education. For those on remand the price has been even higher, with more than one judge accusing prison officers of acting illegally by refusing to take defendants to or from the courts. If the prisons are indeed a chessboard, it is not the officers, despite what some of them may think, who have been the pawns.

CONDITIONS

The most visible manifestation of the crisis in British prisons has been the crisis of conditions. Physical conditions are appalling, particularly in the older prisons. The majority of British prisons were built in the nineteenth century. In England and Wales, of the fifty-five closed prisons in which male inmates were held

---

[42]ibid., 196.
[43]*The Times*, 27 April 1977.
[44]ibid., 7 May 1977.
[45]*Prison Officers' Magazine*, January 1979.

in custody at the end of 1975, only eight have been built as prisons since 1914'.[46] Dartmoor, for example, was built by French prisoners of war in the Napoleonic period; Preston first received offenders in 1799; Cardiff in 1830; Leeds in 1840; Pentonville was built as a 'model' prison in 1842; and Lancaster still has buildings dating back to Norman times. Of the four major prisons in Scotland, Saughton is the most recent addition and was opened in 1926. Peterhead received its first inmates in 1888, Barlinnie in 1882, and Perth in 1842. Together, these Victorian monuments house the majority of people incarcerated in this country.

Overcrowding is rife and endemic, and is frequently presented as the major source of the problems facing the prison service. In February 1980, in England and Wales, 17,093 people were sleeping two or three to a cell designed for one prisoner. As table 1 indicates, cell-sharing is not a recent phenomenon but has been part of prison life for many years.

TABLE 1
OVERCROWDING IN ENGLAND AND WALES[47]

Year	Totals	Three in a cell	Two in a cell
1969	10,539	7,653	2,886
1970	14,174	9,288	4,886
1971	14,450	8,238	6,212
1972	13,737	6,609	7,128
1973	12,609	4,221	8,388
1974	14,146	4,122	10,024
1975	15,640	5,298	10,342
1976	16,435	5,709	10,726
1977	15,990	4,950	11,040
1978	16,098	5,082	11,016
1979	16,585	4,833	11,752
1980 (Feb.)	17,093	5,247	11,486

Overcrowding is particularly evident in local prisons and remand centres, which house short-stay offenders and defendants. In June

---

[46]*Prisons and the Prisoner,* 1977: Paragraph 195.
[47]*Report of the Work of the Prison Department in England and Wales,* 1977, 4; *National Association for the Care and Resettlement of Offenders (NACRO) Factsheet,* 1980.

1980, for example, Winson Green, the local prison in Birmingham, with a total of 596 cells, housed 1,003 prisoners. Strangeways, in Manchester, with 939 places, housed 1,428 prisoners. Brixton, a London remand prison, has accommodation for 696, and in June 1980, held 975 people, while Leeds, with 612 places, accommodated 1,107 people.[48] In Scotland, in June 1979, Barlinnie in Glasgow, with a design capacity of 899 places housed, 1,041 people; Perth with 466 places, housed 552 and Saughton in Edinburgh, with a capacity of 524 places, housed 590 prisoners.[49]

But the statistics, bad as they are, do not show the degrading squalor of two or three people living in a cell designed for one. As Lord Harris, formerly Minister of State at the Home Office, has remarked:

> Those statistics have little meaning until one has entered a small cell in one of our ancient Victorian fortress gaols and seen, and even smelled the effect of these men living together in an oppressive claustrophobic atmosphere.[50]

Many prisoners, particularly those on remand awaiting trial or sentence, spend up to twenty-three hours a day, seven days a week, in such conditions. Norman Fowler, writing in *The Times* in 1971, quoted a prison officer's description of conditions in a 'three'd up' cell:

> It was not until my transfer to the local prison at Gloucester that I encountered this degrading practice and having witnessed it, find it to be abhorrent.
>
> I had occasion, during an evening patrol, to visit an inmate in his cell in order to administer medical treatment. This inmate was sat up in bed, situated behind the door, reading a book. He was attired in pyjamas; his bedding was clean and tidy and he impressed me as being a clean young man. On the wall above him were a few photographs of his family and it was evident that he had been used to living in decent surroundings.
>
> Adjacent to his bunk was a two-tier bunk, occupied by two elderly men. The inmate occupying the top bunk was in bed,

---

[48]*Hansard*, 2 June 1980: Columns 515–16.
[49]*Hansard*, 4 July 1979: Column 623.
[50]*Guardian*, 8 November 1978.

fully dressed, complete with shirt, tie and pullover, and smoking a cigarette. It was obvious that he had not washed. The occupant of the lower bunk was reading, and he too was smoking. By the side of his bed there was a chamber pot, full of urine, with matchsticks and sputum floating on the surface. This, to him, was a convenient spittoon and ashtray.

The cell table was covered in a mixture of salt, sugar, breadcrumbs, spilt tea and tobacco butts. The smell in the room was a combination of 'Black Bell' smoke, stale urine and food rot, and, apart from the small corner where the younger man was lying, the cell was in a filthy condition.

As I entered the cell I was compelled to step back on to the landing because of the stench. On the pretext of looking at the cell board, I was able to inhale some fresh air before venturing into the room again. How that young man must have longed for the privacy of a single cell and what mental suffering he must have endured as he lay in these unhygienic surroundings.

As this prison officer concluded, 'the practice of locating three men in a small cell in a Victorian prison, originally designed to accommodate one, is as barbarous as the treadmill.'[51] A leader article in the *Guardian* seven years later, correctly observed that if 'the prison system came under the health regulations governing shops, factories and offices, the Prison Director would have been taken to court years ago on one of the longest indictments our criminal justice system has witnessed.'[52]

Overcrowding is not a novel feature of prison life. It was first officially acknowledged in the *Report of the Commissioners of Prisons* in 1947. Rather like the old prison hulks adopted as a 'temporary measure' in 1776, and finally abandoned ninety years later, overcrowding was presented in the immediate post-war years as a temporary expedient.[53] Unless there is a radical change in policy, all the present indications are that it will last for more than a (temporary) hundred years.

The impact of overcrowding is not limited to living quarters.

[51] *The Times*, 3 August 1971.
[52] *Guardian*, 31 October 1978.
[53] *Prison Service Journal*, April 1971.

Rather it has a 'knock-on' effect throughout the prisons, and affects workshops, recreation, association, visiting and educational facilities. In such a situation, the fulfilment of the principle of Prison Rule 1 in England and Wales, and Prison Rule 5 in Scotland, which state that the purpose of imprisonment is to help a person to lead 'a good and useful life', becomes even more remote. As the chief director of the Prison Commission in 1962 observed, 'What can you do with 1,700 men [in accommodation for 1,198] except count them, clean them, and lock them up again?'[54]

The situation has recently become even more acute, with the rise in the prison population, which in January 1981 reached 44,600. Moreover, it is important to recognize that the building programme of £500 million announced in 1981 by the Home Secretary[55] is not designed in the first instance to relieve overcrowding, but rather to cope with more prisoners. And even when new facilities are opened, overcrowding continues, as experience at the 'new' Holloway demonstrates. The new women's prison in London has a capacity of 253 prisoners. Between March and May 1978, it held an average of 365 women each day.[56] In June 1980, the prison held 399 women.[57]

Much of the concern about overcrowding is derived from the presumed relationship between the appalling conditions and violence in the prisons. The National Association for the Care and Resettlement of Offenders, for example, has consistently preached the message that unless overcrowding is relieved, there will be more tension and violence. But the relationship is not so obvious. It could be argued that what is remarkable about overcrowded prisons is not the amount of trouble that occurs, but that there is so little. In other words, what is surprising is not that violence can and does happen, but that it should happen so infrequently. The major prison disturbances of the past decade have not been in the short-term, overcrowded, local prisons, but rather in the new long-term institutions such as Gartree and Albany, which are not overcrowded.

---

[54]*Guardian*, 30 April 1962.
[55]*State Research Bulletin*, No. 29.
[56]*The Times*, 1 June 1978.
[57]*Hansard*, 2 June 1980: Column 516.

Overcrowding and the living and working conditions which accompany it are not the central pivot on which the rest of the crisis in prisons is founded. There is no evidence to suggest that if there were hygienic, clean, antiseptic, single-occupant cells throughout the penal system, there would be no crisis. Events at Gartree and Albany have indicated that there is much evidence to the contrary. The significance of the 'crisis in conditions'/is that it reveals the essential bankruptcy of penal policy, and the lack of political will of successive governments to reduce drastically the number of people who serve time in prisons. Seventy-seven per cent of men and ninety per cent of women were sent to prison in England and Wales in 1979 for eighteen months or less.[58] In Scotland, the average length of sentence imposed on men sentenced directly to prison was 224 days and for women 111 days.[59] In addition forty-six per cent of men and forty-seven per cent of women were imprisoned for non-payment of fines.[60] With people on remand, it is these short-termers who bear the brunt of overcrowding. While this may highlight the crisis of conditions, it does not, as frequently suggested, explain either the origins or the nature of the crisis in British prisons.

CONTAINMENT

If there has been a wide-ranging agreement about the dreadful conditions inside the majority of prisons in Britain, particularly in local prisons and remand centres, there has been a sharp polarization of opinion on how to deal with the long-term prisoner. In England and Wales, a long-termer is a man serving over four years, or a woman serving over three years. In Scotland it is anybody serving over eighteen months. In 1979, 18.7 per cent of the average daily male prison population in England and Wales were long-termers.[61] In Scotland, in that year, 43.3 per cent of the average daily male prison population were long-termers.[62]

We will explore the nature and reasons for the growth of long-term

---

[58]*Prison Statistics in England and Wales,* 1979, 55.
[59]*Prisons in Scotland,* 1979, 8.
[60]ibid: Appendix 11.
[61]*Prison Statistics in England and Wales:* Table 1.2.
[62]*Prisons in Scotland,* 1979: Appendix 3.

imprisonment in chapter 4. What concerns us here is the impact of long-termers on the prison system, and the consequent crisis of containment. This particular crisis has revolved around the question of how to cope with people serving such long sentences. From the early 1960s, this question, and the emphasis on control and security which has been the major part of the answer to it, have come to dominate penal thinking and practice. In particular, the escape of a number of top-security prisoners in the mid-1960s was used to justify the beginnings of a security clampdown inside, with all its attendant consequences. This found its first formal expression in the Mountbatten Report on prison escapes and security, published in December 1966. This report was only concerned with England and Wales, but its effects were clearly felt in the Scottish system.

Although the Mountbatten Report is identified as a crucial turning point in recent penal history, the seeds of the security clampdown which followed, and the increasing classification and segregation of prisoners, were already sown. Special maximum security wings had already been introduced before Mountbatten, who commented on conditions in these wings that they were such as 'no country with a record of civilized behaviour ought to tolerate any longer than is absolutely essential as a stop-gap measure'.[63] Since the Mountbatten Report, 'security and control' has become the standard response to explain every feature of prison life. Thus, Leon Brittan, when Minister of State at the Home Office, on being asked in the House of Commons why convicted male prisoners are prevented from wearing their own clothes, replied quite simply: 'To facilitate security and control'.[64]

The full impact of security and control was felt by prisoners in D-wing at Wormwood Scrubs in August 1979. On the third anniversary of the Hull riot, prison officers with staves, shields, visors and helmets attacked 200 prisoners who had been holding a peaceful demonstration. At first the Home Office denied that anybody had been injured, but, again under pressure from PROP, were finally forced to concede that fifty-three had received injuries. In the aftermath of this attack, it was revealed that a 'MUFTI squad' of

---

[63]*Report of the Inquiry on Prison Escapes and Security* (The Mountbatten Report), 1966: Paragraph 212.
[64]*Hansard*, 1 August 1980: Column 789.

prison officers had been used to break up the protest. MUFTI squads [Minimum Use of Force Tactical Intervention], as they are officially labelled, were first used at Gartree in 1978, and at Hull and Styal in 1979, prior to the Wormwood Scrubs incident. The formation of MUFTI squads had never been publicly announced. Nor, until the row about the Scrubs incident had their activities ever been acknowledged.

Since the Mountbatten Report, three features of containment have dominated the prison system; firstly, the pervasive concern with physical security, and the increasingly repressive regimes inside prisons; secondly the increased use of classification, and the segregation of prisoners in special units; finally, the development of new techniques to control the imprisoned population, reflected particularly in the use of drugs.

Central to all these in England and Wales have been the arguments about the policy of dispersing maximum security prisoners throughout the prison system, rather than concentrating them in a single top-security fortress-like prison, as Mountbatten recommended. The policy of dispersal has undoubtedly led to a heightening of tension within the prisons, and advocates of concentration (of whom the prison officers are the most vociferous) are quick to locate the source of recent serious disturbances at Hull, Gartree and Albany prisons, in dispersal policies.

It is also argued, incorrectly we will show later, that dispersal in England and Wales has been the reason for the massive increase in physical security throughout the prison system. New security measures have included the introduction of dog patrols, the use of TV monitoring equipment, use of electronic gates, lights, infra-red cameras for night patrolling, the creation of specialist units of prison officers such as security officers, and extra fences and walls. The impact of these measures has been felt in all areas of prison life, including the availability of visiting, recreational, association and education facilities, the reduction in outside working parties and stricter control and surveillance, not only on the external prison walls and perimeter fences, but within the prison wings and on the cell landings. Thus a person sent down for being drunk and disorderly can find himself guarded by some of the most sophisticated surveillance technology available. As we argue in chapter 4, what is clear is that the crisis of containment stems not from the *nature* but from the *fact* of long-term imprisonment, and it is here that the source of the recent escalating prison protest is to be found.

LEGITIMACY

The final and most crucial aspect of the crisis in British prisons is what we shall refer to as the 'crisis of legitimacy'. As *Prisons and the Prisoner* noted, 'Some people feel that our society should be able to do without prisons',[65] and the calls for the abolition of imprisonment have been heard more frequently in the last ten years. Such calls are based on separate, but related, attacks on the legitimacy of the nature, uses, and role of imprisonment.

In focusing on conditions and containment, for example, we have raised questions about the nature of prisons. Across the political spectrum, vociferous criticism of the conditions inside have been made. Thus, on the one hand, *The Times* has argued that the 'overcrowding in British prisons has become an affront to the efficiency of the penal system . . . The degrading conditions in which some prisoners are forced to live . . . must be disturbing to any civilized community.'[66] On the other hand, organizations such as the National Prisoners' Movement (PROP) have struggled to make visible the realities of penal policies and practices, particularly in the campaign against the attempted cover-up of the Hull disturbance in 1976, and the Wormwood Scrubs one in 1979, and the increasing use of drugs and special units.

But it is on the question of the *role* of prisons that we want to conclude this introduction. To understand the role which imprisonment plays, prisons must be seen within the wider social, political and economic system in which they have been developed. Prisons are a central feature of the debates about crime and punishment, and, more generally, of the efforts to establish, legitimate and maintain social order. The crisis of the British prison system thus reflects not simply a concern about the state of the prisons, but a more widespread belief that the prisons

---

[65]*Prisons and the Prisoner*, 1977: Paragraph 250.
[66]*The Times*, 14 October 1970.

of the State are not making an effective contribution to the maintenance of social order.

Prisons, in principle, operate universally, protecting the freedom, property and life of every individual in the community. But in practice, as we discuss in chapter 6, the sanction of imprisonment is invoked consistently against marginal, lower-class offenders. In so doing, imprisonment serves a class-based legal system, which first, defines the types of social harm which are singled out for punishment, and second, invokes different types of sanctions for different categories of social harm. In this way, for example, most business irregularities are governed by civil rather than criminal law, and are thus subject to milder, restitutive rather than harsher, penal sanctions. Again, middle-class offenders are generally dealt with more leniently than their working-class counterparts, even when they commit similar offences.[67]

Some of the most critical work on prisons in the last few years has been concerned with situating historically the development of the prisons. This work enables us to understand more fully the nature and extent of the prison crisis. We will explore this work in detail in chapter 6. For the moment, it should be recognized that we are arguing for a *political* response to the crisis in British prisons. In particular, we would take issue with those who have sought solutions which are designed solely to improve the operational effectiveness of the prisons. Such solutions are merely partial responses to a more fundamental political crisis which transcends the prison walls.

[67]Schwendinger and Schwendinger, unpublished paper, 14.

2 PRISONS OF THE STATE

The most widely cited aims of the prison system are Prison Rule 1 in England and Wales and Prison Rule 5 in Scotland:

> The purpose of the training and treatment of convicted prisoners shall be to encourage them to lead a good and useful life. (Prison Rule 1, England and Wales)[1]
> The purposes of the training and treatment of convicted prisoners shall be to establish in them the will to lead a good and useful life on discharge, and to fit them to do so. (Prison Rule 5, Scotland)[2]

The sentiments embodied in these rules have their own origin in the 1895 Gladstone Committee report on prisons, which was the first official endorsement of the belief that prisoners are sent to prison not *for*, but *as* punishment, and that efforts should be made to prepare them to lead good and useful lives on their return to the outside world.

One of our central concerns in this book is to explain how and why treatment and training in penal institutions have had such negligible impact. In British prisons the few attempts which have been made to encourage a 'good and useful' life have been either systematically destroyed or cynically subverted.

In this chapter we focus on the tasks of the prison service, its organization and management, and the number and types of prisons

---

[1] *Prison Rules, England and Wales*, 1964: Rule 1.
[2] *Prison Rules, Scotland*, 1952: Rule 5.

and prisoners. A central question we address is how treatment and training, despite its official emphasis, has been subordinated to the demands of containment in general, and of security and control in particular.

It is important to bear in mind that imprisonment does not exist in isolation, but is an integral part of the criminal justice system which has a direct impact on the prisons. For example, the problems of holding increasing numbers of prisoners serving long sentences are a direct outcome of the sentencing policies of the courts. To consider these problems of containment without examining the nature of sentencing policy is to translate a political problem into a 'technical', managerial one. We will explore in chapter 6 the legitimacy of the nature and use of imprisonment, and its political and ideological significance. For the present, our concern is narrower: we seek to describe rather than question who goes to prison and why.

THE TASKS OF THE PRISON SERVICE

Social order does not just happen: it is constantly in the process of being constructed, legitimated, supported and challenged. One of the key elements in this process is the criminal justice system, in which prisons play a crucial role. Officially, the prison service has a number of different but inter-related functions in the criminal justice system. It provides services to the courts; it is responsible for holding in custody those sentenced to deprivation of liberty as a punishment; and it is concerned with the treatment and training of the imprisoned.

The prison service provides three major services to the courts. Firstly, it holds those people accused of criminal offences who have been refused bail and remanded in custody to await trial. Secondly, it holds, and makes reports upon, people who have been convicted but have yet to be sentenced. Thirdly, it has a number of responsibilities for the 'management' of the people being tried. Prison officers, for example, escort remanded prisoners from the prison to the court, staff the cells underneath the court, and, in England and Wales, act as 'Dock Officers' guarding prisoners during the trial. In these ways, prisons are directly involved in the process and administration of criminal justice.

The most visible function of the prison service is the organization and administration of prisons as places of punishment. It is the task of the prison service to contain securely those sentenced to terms of imprisonment. As a former Director of the prison service has written, 'First, the aim is to hold those committed to custody. We can't escape this one.'[3] To hold those imprisoned, the service has developed not only an increasingly complex system of security on the external perimeter walls and fences of the institutions, but also a system of intensive control, surveillance and segregation of prisoners within those walls. In recent years, this concern has become obsessive, and dominates all other aims. A clear illustration of what they refer to as the 'paranoid escalation' about security has been provided by Cohen and Taylor in their description of preparations for the arrival, in 1967, at Durham prison, of three of the 'Great Train Robbers'. This included 'electronic surveillance, dog runs, armed guards, gas masks, and (according to one report) the siting of a machine-gun nest on the external wall.' Troops were called in, and the Chief Constable of Durham crowned the whole affair by observing:

> I am satisfied that Goody's friends were prepared to launch something in the nature of a full-scale military attack, even to the extent of using tanks, bombs, and what the Army describes as limited atomic weapons. Once armoured vehicles had breached the main gates, there would be nothing to stop them. A couple of tanks could easily have come through the streets of Durham unchallenged. Nothing is too extravagant.[4]

As we discuss in detail in chapter 4, this obsession with security has found expression in the increasing uses of physical, psychological and chemical techniques of control.

The primacy of this task of containment has subordinated and subverted the concerns of treatment and training, notwithstanding the aspirations of Prison Rule 1 in England and Wales, and Prison Rule 5 in Scotland. The belief that prisoners should be taught

---

[3]Cited in Fitzgerald, 1977, 16.
[4]Cohen and Taylor, 1972, 16.

how to lead a good and useful life found its first official expression in the Gladstone Committee's report on the prison system in 1895, where it argued:

> The system should be made more elastic, more capable of being adapted to the special cases of individual prisoners; that prison discipline and treatment should be more effectually designed to maintain, stimulate or awaken the higher susceptibilities of prisoners, to develop their moral instincts, to train them in orderly and industrial habits, and whenever possible to turn them out of prison better men and women, both physically and morally, than when they came in.[5]

Since then, each review of the prison system has emphasized these rehabilitative aims. Thus, the 1948 Criminal Justice Act provided that, 'the purpose of training and treatment of convicted prisoners shall be to establish in them the will to lead a good and useful life on discharge, and to fit them to do so'.[6]

But, as has been pointed out frequently, the prison system has consistently and conspicuously failed to rehabilitate offenders. It is curious that the belief in prisons as places of treatment and training has been so widely accepted for so long. It is only in the last few years that the transparency of the myth of rehabilitation has been officially acknowledged. As *Prisons and the Prisoner* observed:

> The coercion which is inherent in a custodial sentence and in the very nature of 'total institutions' tends to direct the whole of the inmates' individual and group energies towards adjustment to the austerely unnatural conditions; towards alienation from authority; and then towards rejection of any rehabilitative goals toward which the staff may be working.[7]

The myths embodied in Prison Rule 1 were finally laid in the May Report which acknowledged that 'the rhetoric of treatment and training has had its day and should be replaced.'[8]

---

[5]*Parliamentary Papers,* Volume 19, 1895, 8.
[6]Cited in Fitzgerald, 1977, 15.
[7]*Prisons and the Prisoner,* 1977: Paragraph 17.
[8]May Report, 1979: Paragraph 4.27.

With the demise of the rehabilitative ideal, and the elevation of security and control to a position of untouchable primacy, the clarion call of penal reform groups has become 'humane containment'. Despite the mounting evidence to the contrary, however, the prison department still believes that there is an important place for a more restricted type of treatment and training in prisons. The aim of staff should now be to 'combine a healthy concern for security and control' with a 'helpful attitude in their *handling* of inmates'[9] (our emphasis). But the dominance of security and control has become extremely unhealthy, and there are few signs of the 'helpful attitudes' in which the prison department places such touching faith.

THE ORGANIZATION OF THE PRISON SYSTEM

The prison system includes not only individual prison establishments, prisoners and staff. There is also an important centralized administration which organizes the service and which has a direct impact and influence on the day to day life of the institutions. It is on this central department (the Home Office in England and Wales, and the Scottish Office in Scotland) that we depend for information about the prisons. Most outside enquiries are directed to these departments, and they control the nature and extent of public knowledge about the prison system.

Constitutionally, Parliament is responsible for the prisons. In England and Wales the Home Secretary, and his or her junior minister, have a direct ministerial responsibility for the work of the Prison Department which is presently housed in the Home Office. The Prison Department includes a Prisons Board, and central staff, four regional offices and the individual penal establishments. The whole organization is headed by the Director-General of the prison service, a senior civil servant.

The Headquarters in London has sixty divisions and sub-divisions, headed by the Prisons Board. The Board is chaired by the Director General, and includes the Deputy Director-General, responsible for the operation of the prison service in the field; a Director of Regimes and Services responsible for planning and co-ordinating prison re-

---

[9] *Prisons and the Prisoner*, 1977: Paragraph 18.

gimes, building programmes, and services; a Director of Operational Policy, responsible for policy and casework on the treatment of prisoners; a Director of Personnel and Finance, responsible for personnel management, industrial relations and staff training as well as manpower and financial control; and a Director of Prison Medical Services. The Board also includes the four regional directors and two non-executive members.[10] The Prison Department also has access to various financial, legal, personnel, administrative, public relations, research and statistical services provided within the Home Office.

Like other parts of the Civil Service, the Prison Department is much criticized for what Cohen and Taylor call 'impersonality, long delays, over-centralization, lack of public accountability of decisions, inscrutability of procedures'. But, as they point out:

> The special nature of the secrecy taboo, the obsession with security and the political sensitivity of the prison issue combine to make the workings of the Prison Department potentially more oppressive than other state bureaucracies.[11]

The Home Office in general, and the Prison Department in particular, is notorious for denying access to information. This has serious consequences not only for outsiders interested in the prisons, but also for prisoners, who find it almost impossible to have their complaints and requests listened to, and acted upon. Wally Probyn, for example, in a perceptive critique of Prison Department responses to prisoners, has recalled:

> The more I challenged the authorities the more I became amazed at the lengths they were prepared to go to oppress me. It seemed that no rule or law was too sacred to violate in order that I should be made to understand that I was outside the law and that it was futile for me ever to try to resolve my grievances by legal means. It occurred to me that one of the reasons that made it impossible for recidivists to reform was that the authorities showed an example of such contempt for law, that

---

[10]*Guardian*, 1 May 1980.
[11]Cohen and Taylor, 1978, 14.

the recidivists could not but take example from this. Furthermore, how does society persuade offenders to respect the rights of others, and to respect a system of law that applies to them only in a punitive form, yet denies them its protection?[12]

In 1980, in response to the criticisms levelled by the May Report, the Home Secretary announced changes to the system of inspection of the prisons. The Chief Inspector of Prisons is to remain a Home Office civil servant, but the inspectorate will no longer be located within the Home Office. The inspectorate is to publish an annual report, reporting directly to the Secretary of State on prison conditions, the treatment of prisoners, and 'such matters as the Secretary of State may direct'.[13] This system of inspection falls well short of the independent inspectorate recommended by May, and will do little to raise the shroud of secrecy which veils the prison system.

For purposes of administration, England and Wales are divided into four regions, Northern, Midlands, South-Eastern and South-Western. Each region is headed by a regional director, and three more deputies. The region is responsible for the application of national penal policy, for the proper functioning of individual establishments, and a number of specialist tasks, including the allocation of prisoners to particular prisons.

Each prison establishment is formally controlled by a governor, who usually has a deputy and a number of assistant governors. It is the governor who is responsible for the day-to-day running of the establishment, and for the maintenance of:

Security, good order and discipline, for the effective co-ordination of the work of all members of its staff, for the regime of the establishment, and the treatment and training of persons in its custody, and for proper use of public money, materials, and premises.[14]

There are more than 500 governors, deputies and assistant

---

[12]Probyn, 1977, 176.
[13]*Guardian*, 1 May 1980.
[14]*Prisons and the Prisoner*, 1977: Paragraph 220.

governors employed in the prison service, including young offender institutions, less than half of whom have come from within the service itself, a source of considerable conflict among prison staff, which we will discuss in chapter 5.

Responsibility for Scottish prisons rests with the Secretary of State for Scotland, and his or her junior minister. The system is centrally organized and administered by the Scottish Home and Health Department within the Scottish Office, based in Edinburgh. Division IIB of the Home and Health Department is the Scottish equivalent of the Prison Department in England and Wales. It is headed by a Director, assisted by an Assistant Secretary, responsible for Administration; an Assistant Controller, responsible for Operations; two Senior Principals, in charge of Establishments and Industries and Supplies; three Principals and six Senior Executive Officers.[15] At the end of 1980, following the recommendation of the May Report, a Chief Inspector for Prisons was appointed for the first time in Scotland.

As in England and Wales, responsibility for the day-to-day running of individual establishments rests with a governor, usually assisted by a deputy and a number of assistant governors. At the end of 1979, there were seventy-five governors, deputies and assistants employed in the Scottish prison service, including young offender establishments.[16]

Relationships in the prison system are rigidly hierarchical. Policies and decisions made at the centre are handed down to those in individual establishments for implementation. Not surprisingly, central directives often meet with hostility and resentment from prison staff, who have been increasingly critical of the central prison departments. And as we have already indicated, a major source of conflict in the prison system is the struggle within the prison service, particularly between staff in headquarters, regions, and individual establishments. As the prison officers' dispute in 1980 made clear, cosmetic changes to the organization of the prison system are largely irrelevant to the increasing tension and conflict between Home Office and Scottish Office administrators, governor grades and uniformed staff.

---

[15] *Scotland's Regions,* 1978, 35.
[16] *Prisons in Scotland,* 1979: Appendix 20.

THE COST OF THE PRISON SYSTEM

Prisons are big business, spending millions of pounds, and employing thousands of people. In a period of economic austerity and severe public expenditure cuts, the spiralling costs of the prison service have provoked much hostile public criticism. In 1979, in England and Wales, £206,731,000 was spent on male prisons and remand centres, and women's establishments. Of this, £152,473,000 was for staffing, including Headquarters staff.[17] In Scotland, the adult prison service cost £19,641,000 of which £15,054,000 was staff costs.[18] In 1978/9, the average weekly cost of keeping a male prisoner inside was £113. This average conceals important variations. For example, the weekly cost of keeping a man in a maximum security dispersal prison was £232, compared with £80 for a man in an open prison. The average cost of keeping a woman in prison during the same period was £140.[19]

At the end of 1976, it was estimated that the cost of building each cell in a new top-security prison was £31,600.[20] Wymott prison, a short-term institution with 816 places, which opened in 1979, cost £10,650,000 to construct. A major new programme of prison building, recommended by the May Report is being planned for the mid-1980s.

Although the new prison building programme will be designed to replace existing institutions rather than simply extending them, evidence from this country and from the USA suggests that without changes in sentencing policy, new facilities will be accompanied by a rise in the prison population. As Michael Zander has observed:

> The American Foundation has shown that the fifteen states that had done most prison building in the past twenty years increased the capacity of their prisons by fifty-six per cent and

---

[17]*Report of the Work of the Prison Department in England and Wales*, 1979: Appendix 4.
[18]*Prisons in Scotland*, 1979: Appendix 21.
[19]*Report of the Work of the Prison Department in England and Wales*, 1979.
[20]*The Times*, 13 December 1978.

their prison population by fifty-seven per cent. The fifteen states that in the same period did the least prison building increased prison capacity by four per cent but decreased their overall prison population by nine per cent.[21]

In the meantime, public expenditure cuts make themselves felt in the already miserably funded areas of education and recreation. Cutbacks in overtime of prison officers has adversely affected visits, letters and association. What little treatment and training there was, is being squeezed out of the system altogether.

TYPES OF PRISON

For official purposes, every adult prison is categorized as either a local prison or a training prison. In 1979, there were twenty-four local prisons and forty-one training prisons in England and Wales.

With the exception of twelve remand cells at Camp Hill for men remanded in custody on the Isle of Wight, all local prisons were originally built in the last century. All are closed prisons, where overcrowding is most severe, and work, educational, visiting and recreation facilities most restricted. Local prisons have a number of functions. They service the courts, holding people remanded in custody to await trial or sentence, and transporting them to and from court appearances. Traditionally, many short-term prisoners have served their time in local prisons, particularly if they are doing six months or less, but in recent years, local prisons have housed increasing numbers of medium and even long-term prisoners. Movement dominates these local establishments; as the Governor of Lincoln remarked, 'I suppose the best way to describe a local prison, possibly rather unkindly, is as a transit camp.'[22]

Training prisons are either open, or closed. In 1979, thirty-two of the forty-one training establishments were of the closed type. The level of security at these prisons varies according to the kind of person being held there. There are seven 'dispersal', maximum security prisons – Parkhurst, Albany, Gartree, Hull, Long Lartin,

[21]*New Society*, 13 December 1979.
[22]BBC Radio, *The Prisoners*, 'The Local Prison', 22 December 1977.

Wormwood Scrubs and Wakefield. In England and Wales, top-security prisoners are not held together in a single institution, but are distributed throughout the dispersal prisons. Officially, a dispersal prison is 'a prison specially organized and equipped to accommodate a proportion of the most dangerous and highest security risk prisoners'.[23] Security and control are at their zenith in these prisons, and there is constant surveillance, counting, checking and re-checking of prisoners.

Training prisons vary in terms of the facilities they offer. Coldingley, for example, was opened in 1969 as the first industrial prison. In the *Visitors' Guide*, Coldingley is described as:

based on the hypothesis that for a certain type of prisoner, the most important part of his training is to learn to work in an efficient, well-managed industrial organization, to have to work under supervision and against the clock in achieving economic levels of output and quality, to earn more or less money according to how hard he works, and his own abilities will allow, and finally, to enjoy the rewards of his own action.[24]

As with other 'specialized' establishments, prisoners are carefully selected for Coldingley, and removed if they fail to fit into the prison regime.

A number of prisons, in practice, cross the divide between 'training' and 'local'. Wormwood Scrubs, for example, is one of the largest prisons in Europe, and is several prisons in one. Each of the four wings has a different function, including a long-term, maximum-security training wing. It also houses the prison hospital for the Southern penal establishments.

The nine open prisons in England and Wales which remained at the beginning of 1979 house the lowest security category prisoners (Category D) and contained less than ten per cent of the adult male prison population. Most are either serving short sentences, or are nearing the end of very long terms. Security might include a wire fence around the perimeter, but usually depends on frequent

---

[23] *Prisons and the Prisoner*, 1977: Paragraph 7.
[24] Caird, 1974, 123-4.

roll-calls. Most are ex-Armed Forces camps; Ford, in Sussex for example was used during the Second World War for parachute training. Within these prisons, the regime is more relaxed than in the local or training establishments and, in particular, prisoners have greater physical freedom of movement. It is the ever-present threat of being sent back to a closed prison, rather than walls and bars, which is used to maintain control within open establishments.

There are four closed prisons for women in England and Wales. The major women's prison, Holloway in London, is in the process of being rebuilt on the original site. In 1979, it had accommodation for 245 but an average daily population of 363, with a maximum of 423. Holloway has a variety of functions, housing remand, short and long-term prisoners. It is a maximum security institution. A wing of Durham prison was recently converted into a top-security unit, with thirty-nine cells for long term, Category A, women prisoners. Effectively, it is a prison within a prison. It has a most sophisticated security system, including electronic locks, cameras and voice-pattern boxes at all points of access to the wing. Styal, in Cheshire, is officially classified as semi-secure. In 1979, it held a daily average of 206 women, with a maximum of 216, in accommodation designed for 173. There are four open prisons for women, together housing a daily average of 383 women.[25] The recent increase in the numbers of women sent to prison led to a change in the role of Cookham Wood. Due to be opened in 1978 as a remand centre for young male offenders, it became an additional establishment for women, and in 1979 housed a daily average of fifty-five women.

There are eleven prisons in Scotland for adult male offenders, and one for women. The categorization between local and training prisons is more blurred in Scotland than in England and Wales, as most prisons contain both short-term and long-term prisoners, kept in separate halls. Edinburgh, for example, houses both local prisoners serving sentences of eighteen months or less, and long-term, first ('star') offenders, while Aberdeen is used for short-term local prisoners, and older, long-term prisoners. Both also hold remand prisoners.

Unlike England and Wales, where they are dispersed in seven

---

[25]*Report of the Work of the Prison Department in England and Wales*, 1979, 71.

prisons, all Category A prisoners in Scotland are housed in Peterhead, the major, long-term, maximum-security establishment, except for six Category A prisoners who, at the end of 1980, were housed in the Special Unit at Barlinnie. Dungavel is an industrial prison, run on similar lines to Coldingley, and designed for 'selected prisoners who, by their behaviour and outlook, are considered suitable for Category C conditions'. There is one small open prison at Penninghame for adult males, with accommodation for sixty-eight prisoners. As in England and Wales, the open prison is used for short-term Category D prisoners, or long-termers nearing the end of their sentence. Again, as in England and Wales, there is the ever-present threat of being sent back to a closed prison if prisoners misbehave. In 1979, nine prisoners were punished by being returned to closed prisons.[26] There is only one prison for women, Cornton Vale, which contains all categories of women prisoners, including remands, and has accommodation for 124.[27]

CATEGORIZATION OF PRISONERS

Prisoners are divided into three main groupings by the prison authorities: prisoners remanded in custody awaiting trial; convicted prisoners remanded in custody awaiting sentence; and convicted, sentenced prisoners. There are also a number of 'civil' prisoners, generally less than two per cent of the daily prison population, imprisoned, for example, under the Immigration Act to await deportation, or for non-payment of rates or maintenance.

In 1979, in England and Wales, 31,316 men were remanded in custody. Of those whose disposal was known at the end of the year, forty-six per cent were found not guilty, not proceeded against or given non-custodial sentences. Similarly, of 2,227 women remanded in custody sixty-eight per cent were either found not guilty, not proceeded against, or given a non-custodial sentence.[28]

In Scotland in 1979, 6,588 men and 438 women were received into custody on remand for either trial or sentence. The annual report *Prisons in Scotland* provides no further breakdown of these figures.[29]

---

[26]*Prisons in Scotland*, 1979, 16.
[27]ibid: Appendix 1.
[28]*Prison Statistics England and Wales*, 1979: Table 2.2.
[29]*Prisons in Scotland*, 1979: Table 2.5.

In Scotland, unlike England and Wales, it is very rare for the time served on remand to be taken into consideration and deducted from a prisoner's sentence. These figures are a clear indication of the punitive use of imprisonment *before* conviction or sentence.

People throughout Britain, when remanded in custody to await trial or sentence, are kept in the prison of the area in which the alleged offence occurred, even if this is far removed from the home of the accused. Officially, 'the intention of the Rules is that while the conditions of their confinement must ensure safe custody and supervision in no less a degree than for convicted prisoners, they should also take account of the fact that they are not convicted'.[30] In practice, living conditions for those remanded are among the worst of any prisoner. The majority live two or three to a cell, locked in for up to twenty-three hours every day. A study by King and Morgan of remand prisoners at Winchester, found that seventy-seven per cent shared three to a cell. There was no association among prisoners, so that, in effect, the remaining twenty-three per cent were held in solitary confinement.[31]

People on remand are allowed certain privileges not granted to a convicted prisoner. For example, all remandees are allowed a daily visit from up to three visitors, except on Sunday. Visits last between twenty and thirty minutes. However, visitors dependent on their fares being paid by the Department of Health and Social Security are only entitled to one supported visit a month. 'Reasonable' facilities are also officially provided for visits from lawyers and solicitors. Such visits take place in the sight but not the hearing of a prison officer.[32] Subject to the governor's discretion, prisoners wear their own clothes, and can receive food parcels from visitors, although parcels are rigorously searched for drugs and escape equipment. They may even 'pay for specially furnished rooms or cells and for certain domestic services', when these are available.[33] In practice, we have been unable to find any examples of this happening. As King and Morgan conclude:

---

[30]*Prisons and the Prisoner,* 1977: Paragraph 168.
[31]King and Morgan, 1976.
[32]*Release,* 1978, 96-7.
[33]*Prisons and the Prisoner,* 1977: Paragraphs 168-9.

Although in principle these conditions may be relieved to some degree by certain privileges in respect of food, letters, visits, newspapers and so on, these are comparatively rarely used, partly because they are out of the financial reach of many unconvicted prisoners. And these privileges are given at the cost of greatly restricted access to facilities which are available to convicted prisoners.[34]

Prisoners on remand do not have to work, and in practice, little work is available even for those who want it. Prisoners on remand are also subject to prison disciplinary proceedings described on page 74, and, since 1973, remandees can be 'awarded' loss of remission to take effect after conviction and sentence.

The daily routine of a prisoner on remand consists of long periods of cell confinement, with short breaks for meals usually taken in the cells, and exercise. A remand prisoner at Lincoln described his daily existence:

In the morning at ten past seven we get unlocked and then it's communal slopping out, we all empty our bowls and chambers from the night before, and then we go down to breakfast, say, about half past seven, fetch our breakfast upstairs, eat it in the cell, get washed, shaved, and then lounge around almost till nine o'clock till they open the doors again and collect our razor blades, and slop out again. And then we're locked up again till eleven o'clock, we'll have half an hour's exercise, come straight in from exercise and have our dinner, go upstairs, collect the mail if there is mail, and then we're locked up again till about ten past two. Then it's slopping out again and then we're locked up again – because there's no work at all – locked up again, as I say, about two o'clock till about half past three. Then we have another half an hour's exercise, lock up again then at four o'clock till perhaps half past four, go down and get our tea, come back, and then we're locked up then until six o'clock, then we slop out again, get rid of our trays and dinner things – er, tea things rather – and then that's it till we're locked up again all night, apart from being out and up for a

---

[34]King and Morgan, 1976, 46.

few minutes for a stop, you know, just to get our buns and tea, and then that's it.[35]

The average length of time a person spends remanded in custody to await trial is increasing. As the Prison Department has acknowledged, 'the time spent in custody by both untried and convicted unsentenced prisoners has increased markedly in recent years.'[36] The period between committal and trial averaged over seventeen weeks in 1979. As the Solicitor-General has pointed out, this national average conceals differences between individual areas 'so wide as to render it quite unintelligible'. In the first nine months of 1979, for example, the average waiting time in London between committal and trial was 18.8 weeks.[37] For individuals, the wait can be well over a year. At the end of January 1980, for example, two women had been held on remand awaiting trial for drug offences for 440 days.[38] On 1 May 1980, a prisoner had been awaiting trial for 561 days.[39] On 10 June, a man, who had been remanded in custody for a total of 600 days, was discharged from court after the prosecution formally offered no evidence.[40]

Prisoners on remand frequently experience great personal hardship. They risk losing their jobs, encountering severe financial difficulties, and putting great stress on their personal relationships. There is little likelihood of receiving any compensation if they are found not guilty. Although people in Britain are legally innocent until proven guilty, the nature and conditions of remands in custody to await trial clearly illustrate the principle that underlies the accusations levelled against the remanded: 'Convicted until proven innocent'.

SENTENCED PRISONERS

The majority of people sentenced to imprisonment receive short

[35]BBC Radio. *The Prisoners*, 'The Local Prison' 22 December 1977.
[36]*Prison Statistics, England and Wales*, 1979, 26.
[37]*Hansard*, 26 February 1980: Columns 494-5.
[38]*Hansard*, 27 March 1980: Column 523.
[39]*Hansard*, 19 June 1980: Column 607.
[40]*Hansard*, 23 June 1980: Columns 19-20.

sentences. During 1979, in England and Wales, 31,023 men were received into prison under sentence of immediate imprisonment, and a further 13,132 were received for non-payment of fines. The number of people sentenced to imprisonment has increased annually since 1974. The largest increase has been of people sentenced to six months or less. Forty-three per cent of men sentenced to imprisonment in 1979 received sentences of six months or less.[41]

In the same year, 1,800 women were sentenced to immediate imprisonment, and 726 were committed to prison for non-payment of fines. The use of imprisonment is increasing for women, as it is for men, and again the biggest increase is of those sentenced to over three months and less than six months. In 1979, of all the women who received prison sentences sixty-two per cent were sentenced to six months or less. (In 1975, the comparable figure was fifty-one per cent).[42]

This extensive use of short-term imprisonment is masked in the average daily prison population. While the total number received into prison in any one year is large, short-termers make up a small proportion of the total prison population at any one time. The average daily, adult prison population in 1979 in England and Wales was 'higher than any previous level reached this century'.[43] It can be categorized as in tables 2 and 3.

TABLE 2
AVERAGE DAILY ADULT CRIMINAL MALE PRISON
POPULATION (ENGLAND AND WALES), 1979

	Number	*Per cent*
Untried	2615	9.2
Convicted awaiting sentence	1039	3.7
Less than eighteen months	8489	29.7
Eighteen months	2346	8.3
Over eighteen months and up to four years	8594	30.3
Over four years and up to ten years	3548	12.5
Over ten years (excluding life)	459	1.6
Life	1314	4.6

Source: *Prison Statistics, England and Wales*, 1979: Table 1.2.

---

[41]*Prison Statistics, England and Wales*, 1979, 49.
[42]*Prison Statistics, England and Wales*, 1979, 55.
[43]*Prison Statistics, England and Wales*, 1979, 9.

TABLE 3

AVERAGE DAILY ADULT CRIMINAL FEMALE PRISON
POPULATION (ENGLAND AND WALES), 1979

	Number	*Per cent*
Untried	121	12
Convicted awaiting sentence	71	7.1
Less than eighteen months	431	42.8
Eighteen months	88	8.7
Over eighteen months and up to three years	164	16.3
Over three years and up to ten years	85	8.4
Over ten years (excluding life)	4	0.4
Life	43	4.3

Source: *Prison Statistics, England and Wales*, 1979: Table 1.2.

As in England and Wales, the majority of men and women sentenced to imprisonment in Scotland are short-termers. In 1979, over ninety per cent of people imprisoned by the courts received sentences of eighteen months or less. Moreover, of 10,452 men sent to prison in 1979, 4,824 were sent for non-payment of fines.[44] The average length of sentence in Scotland was 140 days (excluding life). Again, the extent of the use of short-term imprisonment in Scotland is disguised in the average daily prison population, which is made up as shown in table 4.

All prisoners are further categorized by length of sentence. In England and Wales, men serving eighteen months or less are short-termers; over eighteen months and less than four years, medium-termers; and over four years, long-termers. Women serving three years or less are categorized as short-term, and those doing over three years are long-termers. In Scotland, men and women serving eighteen months or less are short-term; over eighteen months, long-term.

When considering length of sentence, it is important to bear in mind that prisoners serving thirty days or over are entitled to have one-third of their sentence remitted for good behaviour. This system

---

[44]*Prisons in Scotland*, 1979: Appendix 1.

TABLE 4

AVERAGE DAILY ADULT PRISON POPULATION IN
SCOTLAND, 1979

	Men		Women	
	Number	*Per cent*	*Number*	*Per cent*
Untried	541	17.2	25	27.5
Convicted awaiting sentence	120	3.8	5	5.5
Less than one month	174	5.5	11	12.1
One month and less than three months	263	8.3	10	11.0
Three months and less than six months	279	8.8	10	11.0
Six months and less than eighteen months	410	13.0	14	15.4
Eighteen months and less than two years	175	5.5	3	3.3
Two years and less than three years	192	6.1	2	2.2
Three years and over (excluding life)	733	23.2	7	7.7
Life	267	8.5	4	4.4

Source: *Prisons in Scotland,* 1979: Appendix 3.

of remission as it is known, is an important method of ensuring conformity to prison rules, as we later show on page 101. Misbehaviour is frequently punished by loss of remission. Entitlement to remission is a privilege, not a right, and, theoretically, prisoners who had served two-thirds of their sentence and not lost any remission, could be held to complete their full sentence. There is no system of remission for prisoners serving life.

CLASSIFICATION OF PRISONERS

As well as being categorized by age, sex, and status (untried, convicted but unsentenced, sentenced, civil), prisoners are also classified. All those sent to prison, either on remand or convicted are sent to the local prison or remand centre serving the court from which they were committed, or at which they have been charged.

Observation and classification units exist in all local prisons, and 'assess' people serving three months or more. For men sentenced to four years or over, in England and Wales, the assessment takes place at regional allocation centres in local prisons at Liverpool, Birmingham, Wandsworth, Wormwood Scrubs and Bristol. In Scotland, assessment of men serving over eighteen months takes place in Saughton prison, Edinburgh.

Assessment in Britain has four main aims:

(a) to obtain and record certain basic information about each prisoner and about his family background;
(b) to attempt to identify his needs and, if possible, the factors that may have led to his criminal behaviour, as an essential preliminary to any attempt to deal with him while he is in custody;
(c) to settle his security category;
(d) in the light of these factors, and of the resources available to the region, to recommend where he should serve the whole or first part of his sentence.[45]

Officially, assessment is directly linked to the 'treatment and training ' of prisoners. It is 'a positive method of ensuring that so far as possible each inmate is placed in a group in which he will receive the treatment and training most appropriate to his individual aptitudes and needs'.[46] The impetus for such classification for treatment came from the Gladstone Committee of 1895, which considered that the possibilities of successful rehabilitation 'would largely be increased by a careful classification of prisoners'.[47]

Prior to 1895, classification had been used as a basis for segregating prisoners for security and control purposes, and as one writer has concluded:

It is doubtful whether the basic administrative and management concerns which emerge from a study of the historical development of classification, have lost much of their over-riding influence on the process, even though the criteria

---

[45]*Prisons and the Prisoner,* 1977: Paragraph 30.
[46]ibid: Paragraph 26.
[47]*Parliamentary Papers,* Volume 19, 1895, 9.

and justifications for these concerns may have become somewhat more sophisticated with the passage of time.[48]

This historical primacy of administrative and management concerns can be seen clearly both in the nature of the classificatory system presently used, and in the reasons for its adoption. The scheme was proposed by the Mountbatten *Report of the Inquiry into Prison Escapes and Security,* published in December 1966, in the wake of the escape of a number of highest security prisoners. It was thus security, not treatment and training, which was the rationale for the four-tier classification system which Mountbatten proposed:

Category A: Prisoners whose escape would be highly dangerous to the public or police or to the security of the state;

Category B: Prisoners for whom the very highest conditions of security are not necessary but for whom escape must be made very difficult;

Category C: Prisoners who cannot be trusted in open conditions, but who do not have the ability or resources to make a determined escape attempt;

Category D: Those who can reasonably be trusted to serve their sentences in open conditions.[49]

This system, based entirely on security risk, was immediately accepted and adopted by the prison departments in England and Wales and Scotland. This unquestioning acceptance indicates how far security and control have subordinated the aims of treatment and training to 'a very poor second, despite what many people might wish to believe and what most official statements have been proclaiming for many years'.[50]

On reception into prison, each prisoner will be assessed for

---

[48]Bottomley, 1973, 181.

[49]*Report of the Inquiry into Prison Escapes and Security* (Mountbatten Report): Paragraph 217.

[50]Bottomley, 1973, 185.

classification as Category A, B, C or D. Prisoners have no right to know why they are allocated to one category rather than another. From time to time, during a sentence, the category will be examined, and a prisoner can be either upgraded or downgraded. In both England and Wales and Scotland, all decisions about Category A prisoners, including initial allocation of the category, and the occasional review, are taken centrally in the Prison Departments.

On 1 February 1980, 283 men and seven women were classified Category A in England and Wales.[51]

Category A prisoners are subject to a whole series of restrictions over and above those already contained in the prison rules. For example, all their visitors are vetted by the police. Potential visitors are visited by the police and must submit two photographs and other personal details to the prison department. The ruling that visitors should be close relatives or known to the prisoner before conviction is rigorously enforced, and in some cases only immediate family are allowed to visit. Category A prisoners can be denied classes, trade training courses, and recreation facilities. They must leave their clothes outside their cells at night, and must wear rubber soled shoes. The cell light burns twenty-four hours a day. All movements of Category A prisoners within a prison must be dated, timed, described and signed in a log book carried by the prison officer escorting the prisoner, a system described by one Category A man as 'the ultimate stage in dehumanization'.[52] Such restrictions are not embodied in the Prison Rules, but were introduced and are altered by administrative fiat at the discretion of the prison authorities.

In England and Wales, there is also a supplementary Category E, which is for prisoners who have either attempted to, or actually escaped. For Category B prisoners, an escape or escape attempt may mean reclassification as Category A. Category E prisoners are subject to a special watch, wear prison clothes with yellow patches, and have all letters and visits closely monitored. The governors of individual institutions have discretion about the allocation to, or time served on Category E.[53]

Prisoners in Category A cannot be released without first being

[51]Hansard, 8-14 February 1980: Column 218.
[52]Probyn, 1977, 171.
[53]*Release*, 1978, 94.

re-classified. In Scotland, the system of reclassification known as 'up-grading' may involve transferring from one prison to another. For prisoners being re-classified prior to release, the experience of being 'upgraded' can be frustrating:

> He may have to share a cell or dormitory with other prisoners after having been in the 'privacy' of a single cell for anything up to ten years. This is not an easy transition for many prisoners to make.
>
> He may find rules and regulations enforced more strictly in the prison he is being 'upgraded' to. For example, he may have to get a haircut, he might have to walk in single file, he might not be allowed into a friend's cell during recreation time.
>
> He might have rigorous cell inspections for the first time in his sentence. He almost certainly will have to move through the hall system again. That is: from the 'best' hall in Perth he will be upgraded to the 'worst' hall in Edinburgh. It will then be up to him to 'prove himself', to show he is worthy of moving up through the hall system to the 'best' hall again. (Although we can assume that he has already 'proved himself' or he would not have been upgraded in the first place.) In short, 'upgrading', instead of being progressive and continuous, is like a series of steps where each step means returning practically to stage one.[54]

If a prisoner 'fails to adjust' at any stage, he can be 'downgraded', and be made to go through the whole process again.

Remand prisoners too can be held under Category A conditions. Women held as Category A on remand are kept in solitary confinement in Brixton male prison.

One group within Category A merits special attention – the Irish prisoners. In 1979, there were eighty convicted Republican prisoners in England and Wales, of whom twenty-eight were serving life sentences with minimum recommendations of thirty years or over, and thirteen who were serving fourteen years or over. All Republican prisoners are classified as Category A, even those serving six years or less. Fifty-five of the eighty have families in Ireland, many of whom

---

[54]MacDonald and Sim, 1978, 22.

find it almost impossible to visit them. The social security services of both the Republic of Ireland and Northern Ireland do not provide funds for members of families to come over to England to visit imprisoned relatives. There is thus 'an effective financial barrier to members of the family visiting relatives serving sentences of imprisonment in England and Wales, where those families reside outside England and Wales.'[55]

When visits do occur, they take place under rigorous security. Both prisoner and visitors, including children, can be subject to a strip search before and after the visit. Prison officers sit next to both prisoner and visitor, taking note of, and sometimes interrupting the conversation. Visits are always 'closed' and take place either with a screen of wire-reinforced glass or a partial hardboard partition separating prisoner and visitor, or in a separate room, often a converted cell. The prisoner and visitors sit on opposite sides of a table, with a prison officer sitting at the side of the same table. A second prison officer will also be in the room, and others posted outside. No physical contact of any description is allowed.

Irish prisoners, with four notable exceptions, have not been allowed transfers to prisons in Northern Ireland to make visiting easier. This refusal by the Home Office should be understood in the context of a policy which permits civilians and servicemen convicted of criminal offences in Northern Ireland to return to England to serve their sentences. Between 1972 and 1975, twenty-two civilians and twenty-six servicemen were transferred from Northern Ireland to England.[56]

Irish prisoners have complained consistently about visiting conditions, and the refusal to transfer them. In November 1975, for example, Irish prisoners demonstrated on the rooftops of Wormwood Scrubs, and others have gone on hunger strikes. Similar protests have been made against enforced solitary confinement, extensive censorship of newspapers and books which Irish prisoners are permitted, and the refusal of the Home Office to permit some Irish prisoners to write to solicitors about possible legal action over physical injuries allegedly received while being held before trial.[57]

---

[55]Logan, 1976, 41.
[56]ibid.
[57]ibid.

LIFE PRISONERS

In England and Wales, male prisoners sentenced to life imprisonment have been subject to a separate system of classification since 1975. Murder is the only crime for which a life sentence is mandatory, but an increasing number of people have been sentenced to 'life' for non-homicidal offences, including violence, rape, arson and buggery. The number of life sentence prisoners has steadily increased. At the end of 1979, there were 1,463 men and fifty women serving 'life' in England and Wales.[58] In Scotland, 364 men and four women were serving life sentences (including orders to be detained during Her Majesty's Pleasure).[59]

The average time served on a life sentence was nine years eight months in 1979. However this average conceals the range of time served, which varied from two years seven months in one case, to over twenty years in another, during the period 1975-9.[60] On 31 August 1979, in England and Wales, 881 people were serving sentences imposed over five years previously, of whom 232 were serving sentences imposed over ten years previously. Seven people had been in custody continuously for twenty years or more.[61]

Life prisoners are first sent to special assessment units at either Wormwood Scrubs or Wakefield. They spend their first few days in the prison hospital under observation. During the first four months, a prisoner is assigned to a prison officer, with whom he is expected to develop a 'special relationship', and attends group therapy sessions designed to help him come to terms with his sentence. At the end of three years, he will be allocated to another prison, after a major review of his progress. Throughout these earlier years, the prisoner is closely monitored by the staff, including a prison psychologist and a prison doctor.

It is clear that this policy is not working out in practice. Moreover the 'new policy of itself does not tackle the real problem: why the

---

[58]*Report of the Work of the Prison Department in England and Wales,* 1979: Paragraph 55.
[59]*Prisons in Scotland,* 1979, 11.
[60]*Hansard,* 18-24 January 1980: Column 106.
[61]*Hansard,* 2-8 November 1980: Column 244.

number of life imprisonment sentences in Britain is so different to that of other countries'.[62]

Classification in British prisons has little to do with treatment and training. Rather, it is based upon, and directed towards the demands of security, control, segregation, and allocation. Indeed, as this chapter has shown, the whole prison system is structured upon and informed by the demands of containment and control. It is hardly surprising then that the May Committee found that most of the comments it received on the purposes of imprisonment were 'unsystematic and rarely precise'.[63] But then the official purposes have never had any real impact on the organization and management of the prison system.

[62]*Sunday Times,* 2 November 1975.
[63]May Report, 1979: Paragraph 427.

3 PEOPLE IN PRISON

Chapter 2 was about what might be called the 'quantitative' aspects of imprisonment – the number and types of prison and prisoner, and the organization and finance of the penal system. This chapter explores the 'qualitative' aspects of imprisonment – what happens to the incarcerated, the conditions in which they are held, and particular features of prison life. Quantitative and qualitative aspects are closely inter-related. Severe overcrowding, particularly in local prisons, has a direct impact on the quality of life inside these establishments, but the statistical significance of three to a cell is lost without an understanding of the conditions in which those three people have to live.

But such conditions are not simply a result of overcrowding. If single cells were provided for every prisoner tomorrow, major problems would still confront the prison system, as the recent disturbances at Albany, Gartree and Hull, which were not overcrowded, make clear. Overcrowding might exacerbate, but it does not in itself either cause or explain the crisis of conditions.

In this chapter we outline and illustrate day to day life inside British prisons. Beginning with the reception into prison of a convicted prisoner, we trace 'a day in the life of' a prison and its prisoners, and focus on particular aspects of that day – on work, education, letters and visits, discipline and medical facilities. Conditions vary from institution to institution, and within institutions over time, and so we draw a typified picture, using specific examples to illustrate general themes and issues.

RECEPTION

Reception is the machine through which people are processed and fed into the prison system. It symbolizes the passage from 'freedom' to incarceration, and involves an explicitly simple, but implicitly complex process of changing people from citizens to prisoners. The nature of reception is bureaucratic: a citizen's identity is transferred on to forms and into boxes to be held until the whole process is reversed, and the prisoner becomes a citizen again.[1]

Immediately on arrival in the prison, prisoners are escorted into the reception area. They sit on long, wooden benches, waiting for their surnames to be called. When called, they step forward and give their name, address and personal possessions to a prison officer who notes down the information, and boxes the personal effects. The prisoner signs an inventory of his belongings. Taken into an adjoining room, prisoners are ordered to remove all clothing, and to shake them to ensure no contraband is hidden in the folds. Each prisoner is given a pair of underpants, socks and a prison shirt, is weighed, measured, and directed into the bath-house, where he washes in a few inches of tepid water. Meanwhile, a prisoner working in the reception area sizes up the new arrival for a uniform. With the smells and dirt of the outside world removed, the prisoner dresses. Standard prison uniform consists of 'grey serge trousers, blue and white striped shirt, grey serge lapel-less jacket, grey socks, thick-soled, lace-up shoes, and a breakable blue tie'. All these items are at least second hand, and ill-fitting. Prisoners are not allowed to adjust uniforms to make them more comfortable to wear. To do so is a punishable offence. As Rod Caird observed:

> It does nothing to reassure the prisoner that he is, after all, a person, and not just a 'con'. It is not only a uniform, with all the feeling of regimentation and sameness which that entails but also a *shabby*, degrading uniform.[2]

Each prisoner also receives a blunt knife, fork, spoon, plastic plate, plastic mug and pillow case.

---

[1]Caird, 1974, 10-12.
[2]ibid.

Suitably clothed, the prisoner is finger-printed, photographed and 'medically examined'. This examination is brief and to the point:

> An officer came in and told us to take off our shirts, and we were called one by one before the doctor, who was standing behind what looked like a church lectern, with an officer behind him watching:
> 'Are you fit?'
> 'Yes.'
> 'That's all then.'[3]

On the basis of this examination, the prisoner is declared fit for work.

Throughout the whole process, contact between officers and prisoners is minimal. Orders are given to be taken without explanation. Prisoners who ask questions are quickly reminded that this is prison, where you do what you are told, and don't ask why. In the penal system, orders are many, and explanations are rare. Reception is the first contact with this for new prisoners, and it is designed to make a lasting impression. While there is often frantic activity in the reception area as a whole (due to the large number of people being processed) the pace of processing each individual is slow, and allows plenty of time for the numbness which often follows sentencing to begin to wear off. For the bewildered first-timers, out of the noisy chaos of reception comes the clear message that they are now the property of the prison authorities. No longer citizens, but prisoners; processed, packed, numbered and ready for grading and entry into the main part of the prison, the property of the state.

CELLS

Having been received into the institution, prisoners are escorted to the cells. Each door they enter is systematically unlocked and locked, a feature of prison life to which the first-timer will soon become accustomed. Closed prisons are divided up into wings or halls. Each has a number of levels or landings, containing the cells. The number of cells on each tier varies from prison to prison, and from wing to

---

[3]ibid., 12-13.

wing. At Barlinnie in Glasgow for example, there are sixty cells on each of the four levels. Each level is supervised by a 'gallery' or 'landing' officer, responsible to the principal officer in charge of the wing. The landings are constructed to enable one officer to see everything that is happening outside the cells. Landings are rectangular, and in some prisons, wire meshing covers the open space between them to prevent people or objects being thrown down onto the floor below. Many older prisons, for example Pentonville and Wandsworth, were built in the form of a star, with different wings radiating from a common administrative centre. Movement on any of the landings or any wing can be monitored from this central point.

On entering the wing, prisoners are lined up and each individual is formally handed over by the reception officer to the wing's principal officer or his deputy. Prisoners are handed the basic necessities for living in the cells, including towels, sheets, wash-things, toothbrush, toothpowder, chamber-pot, water-jug and plastic basin. And then, as if to make the change of status complete, prisoners are handed their new identities on a cell-card; surname, prison number, length of sentence, court from which they have come, cell number, and earliest date of release. Religious affiliation is shown by the colour of the card.

Prisoners are then taken to their cells. Cell sizes vary: the dimensions of a traditional cell in England and Wales are eleven feet by twelve feet by seven feet, and in Scottish prisons, ten feet by seven and a half feet.[4] Cells in both England and Wales and Scotland have a tiny barred window on one wall, which a prisoner can look out of only by standing on a chair. The heavy metal door can only be opened from the outside, and has an aperture or peep-hole for surveillance. On the outside of the door is a small frame for the cell card. Ventilation is minimal. Cell walls are bare, and the bricks are roughly painted, and scrawled on. A bare light is fixed into the ceiling, casting a dull shadow in the cell. Headaches and eye strain are common. The light switch is on the wall outside the cell, and is switched on and off by the landing officer. In most prisons lights are out by ten o'clock in the evening. There is a bell in each cell, which prisoners can ring and call the landing officer.

Within each cell, there is a bed, table, chair, picture board, and

---

[4]*Prisons and Other Penal Establishments in Scotland,* 1978, 4.

small cupboard. There is no fixed sanitation. Prisoners use the chamberpot, or 'piss pot' for urinating and defecating, emptying the pots once a day in the early morning. For prisoners sharing a cell (the majority in local prisons and remand centres), each cell will have a double bunk, a single bed, two tables, up to three chairs, three plastic washbowls, three plastic water jugs, and three piss-pots. At any one time there is only room for one prisoner to move around the cell. In the most recently built prisons, where cells are smaller, a prisoner estimated that there was ground-floor space in his cell to move around in equivalent to two telephone kiosks.

Heating is piped into the cells, and cannot be regulated by the prisoner. In the older prisons, in particular, the heating frequently malfunctions. In winter people often sleep with their clothes on, to try and keep warm in the dank atmosphere. In summer, they sit almost naked, sweating profusely.

For many prisoners, especially those on remand, twenty-three hours a day are spent in their cells. In many older prisons where work is provided, it is occasionally done in the cells and meals are usually eaten there. At the end of each landing is a recess with sinks and toilets. These facilities are so spartan that prisoners have to 'slop out' their plastic chamber pots in strict rotation to prevent the drainage system clogging up. As is characteristic of imprisonment, privacy is minimal: even the toilets in the recess have saloon-type doors, so that prisoners can be watched.

Apart from their physical features, and the cramped nature of the living accommodation, the smell is the most outstanding feature of the cells and landings. When three people live together, urinate and defecate, eat meals, work, while away hour after hour, day after day, being able to take a quick shower or bath and change their clothes and bedding only once a week at most, a smell is produced which contaminates the physical surroundings and permeates individual prisoners. It is in these conditions that many prisoners live out their sentences.

A DAY IN THE LIFE OF . . .

The daily routine varies from institution to institution. At worst, people are locked in their cells all day and night, only getting out to 'slop out' and take exercise (weather permitting). Each morning about six o'clock, and after the first count of the day, the cells are unlocked. In the next two hours, they 'slop out', wash, make their beds, clean the cells, and eat breakfast. 'Slopping out' is one of the most symbolic practices of modern prison life. Prisoners carry their piss-pots down the landing, and queue up to empty them in the recess. Although chamber pots are supposed to be used to defecate, most prisoners prefer to wrap excrement up in newspaper and drop it out of their cell windows. The risk of being punished for this breach of prison rules is preferable to enduring the smell day and night. A group of prisoners are officially employed to walk round the outside of the wings collecting the bundles of papers. Sanitary facilities in many prisons are so overloaded that recesses are frequently flooded sometimes to the extent that urine drains out over the landing and down the walls. Prisoners refill their jugs with water and either wash and shave at the recess, or, more usually, go back to their cells to do this. Razor blades are handed out and collected back each morning. If a prisoner wishes to grow or shave off a moustache or beard he has to seek permission from the governor. Applications to see the governor, doctor or social worker must be made during this period. Applications are made through the principal officer who decides whether or not a prisoner will see the governor.

Before eight o'clock, prisoners who are going to workshops line up outside their cells. They are counted out of the wing, marched over and counted into the workshop. At midday, they are counted out of the workshop and marched back into the wing or dining hall for dinner. They are counted again. Exercise is taken immediately after lunch, weather permitting. For many this consists of walking in twos and threes round and round a circular path on the exercise yard, under the surveillance of prison officers, and in some prisons in England and Wales, dogs.

(Dogs are not used in Scottish prisons. At the 1978 Scottish Prison Officers' Association Conference, a motion to introduce dogs into the Scottish Prison Service was supported, although the Executive informed delegates that 'since dogs had been employed in (English) prisons they had bitten more staff than inmates.')[5]

An hour's walk later, prisoners are taken back into the wings.

---

[5] *Scotsman*, 18 March 1978.

Again they line up for work and are counted both out of the wing and into the workshop. Work ends about five o'clock and prisoners are counted and marched back to either cells or the dining room for tea. Whenever they move out of the workshops, they are searched, and every tool must be accounted for before prisoners are allowed to leave. When moving from one part of the prison to another prisoners are always escorted and formally handed over to the officer in charge. After tea, prisoners are usually locked in their cells for a 'quiet hour', which is historically provided as a space for personal reflection. It also coincides with the time staff take tea.

In the early evening, prisoners may be unlocked for a recreation period, when they can associate with others, attend evening classes, watch television, read papers, and play games such as darts, snooker, chess, and table tennis where facilities exist. In Barlinnie, for example, there is a separate recreation hall with two table tennis tables, two snooker tables and two dart boards for as many as 150 men. The majority either stay in their cells, watch television or simply walk around the hall area, talking with friends. Only prisoners serving six months or over are permitted recreation. In many prisons there are no separate recreation facilities outside the wing, and in some prisons, prisoners are not allowed to meet in individual cells.

By about nine o'clock prisoners are back in their cells for supper (tea and a bun). Officers begin to lock up, counting as they go from cell to cell. About ten o'clock the lights go out. Throughout the night, the patrolling officer will look through the peep-hole of each cell to check that the occupants are inside asleep. For top security prisoners, the cell light burns all night.

The routine in Barlinnie is typical of the routine for most prisoners in Britain during the week. At weekends, there is no work for the majority, and the prisoners spend long hours locked up in their cells. As we have said, different prisons with different facilities will operate a variety of regimes. For example, in some prisons lights go out at 8.30 p.m., while in others individual prisoners can have their lights on until midnight. But the overall pattern remains constant. Throughout the day and night, there is continual surveillance and counting. In all prisons, during the day it is very noisy, with the slamming of doors, shuffling of feet, clinking of keys and shouting of orders down vacuous halls. Even at night, the movement of officers and the ringing of cell bells by prisoners wanting to attract the officer's attention punctuate the quieter atmosphere.

Overall, the most striking feature of daily life in prison is the routinized boredom of people passing rather than spending time.

FOOD

One of the oldest and commonest complaints made by prisoners is about food. Officially, food is one of the basic elements of the prison regime, and the statutory rules require it to be 'wholesome, nutritious, well-prepared and served, reasonably varied, and sufficient in quantity'.[6]

In February 1980, the prison authorities contrived to fulfil these requirements by spending 59 pence per day, per prisoner, on food[7] – less than they spent on feeding the prison dogs. At the discretion of the governor, special diets can be authorized on medical or religious grounds.

Rod Caird has described the food in Coldingley:

There are three main meals in the day, with an 'evening drink' just before lights out. Breakfast consists of the inevitable porridge, something cooked (perhaps a rasher of bacon), four slices of bread and a dollop of margarine. Lunch is the sort of meal which is served up in many institutions – starchy, cabbagey, and tasteless, but not actually unpleasant. Apart from the odd bug in the cabbage, the food is mostly clean. Tea is rather like breakfast without the porridge; of course, half pint mugs of sugarless tea accompany most meals. One tablespoonful is dished out at breakfast: enough to sweeten the tea or the porridge properly, or both of them slightly. A difficult decision with which to start the day.

The weekends bring with them special food – cornflakes on Saturday mornings, an apple and a piece of cheese at tea-time, with perhaps some marmalade on Sunday morning. In view of

---

[6]*Prisons and the Prisoner,* 1977: Paragraph 39.
[7]*Hansard,* 15-21 February 1980: Column 646.

this monotonous diet it is hardly surprising that most prisoners rapidly take on a pasty, puffy appearance.[8]

Meals are usually served lukewarm, whether taken in the dining hall, or in the cells. Prisoners eating in their cells usually have to queue up and collect meals in the wing and take them back up to their cells. Meals are often served on tin trays, which have separate compartments for each course, although at Wandsworth, for example, only the midday meal is served on a tray. Other meals are served on plastic plates, kept by the prisoner. For most prisoners, there is little choice or variation of menu. It is widely believed by prisoners that some of the food sent in for them never gets beyond the kitchen doors. For both prisoners and prison officers, working or supervising in the kitchens is said to be a lucrative business.

WORK

Prisons are officially both places of punishment and rehabilitation. These goals are not necessarily regarded as being in opposition to each other, and both can be found in the same activity or routine. This is particularly true of work. Under the statutory rules, employment must be provide for all people over school age who are fit to work, and it is a punishable offence to refuse to work.

In England and Wales, prison industries have been organized under 'Prindus', the 'corporate identity' given to them in 1972 which:

> symbolizes the belief that industrial experience in a realistic working environment benefits those in custody and the public interest. The offender is less alienated from the outside world if he does a regular job in prison. And the community gains because he is more readily assimilated on release.[9]

The development of Prindus was hailed by the then Minister of

---

[8]Caird, 1974, 39.
[9]*Prindus First Catalogue,* 1972: Inside cover.

State at the Home Office, Lord Colville, as a 'significant step' in the organization of work inside. He estimated that within five years there would be 26,000 prisoners producing products worth £18 million, and making a profit of £1,750,000.[10] In fact, in 1979, prison industries lost £4,700,000.[11]

Prison work is classified into industry, farming, works, domestic duties, outside work and full-time education (including vocational and trade training). In 1979, in England and Wales, 12,282 men were employed in industry. This included laundry work, tailoring, textiles (including sewing mailbags), and woodwork. While some of the newer prisons have more modern facilities, workshops in older prisons remain generally overcrowded, and conditions are very poor, with inadequate heating, lighting, ventilation, and work space. Most of the work done is notable for being boring, repetitive and lacking in any sort of skill. In 1976 the second largest single task in industrial work was sewing and repairing mailbags, which was the job of 2,756 male prisoners.[12] However, the 1977 Report was able to proclaim a 'minor landmark ' with the 'phasing out of the familiar canvas mailbag in favour of a polypropelene product'.[13] In 1979, sixty-three per cent of all industrial workshop produce was 'bought' by the prison department itself. This included furniture, fittings, and uniforms for prisoners and prison staff. Of the remainder, sixteen per cent was sold to other government departments (for example, road signs, stationery), and twenty-one per cent was work undertaken for outside sales.[14]

Farming employed 1,589 men in 1979. The prison department:

owns and rents about 17,000 acres of land of which about 4,500 acres are sites of prison buildings and staff quarters and sites for new establishments; about 11,000 acres are used for the

---

[10]*The Times*, 11 November 1972.

[11]*Report of the Work of the Prison Department in England and Wales*, 1979: Paragraph 110.

[12]*Report of the Work of the Prison Department in England and Wales*, 1976: Table 10.5.

[13]*Report of the Work of the Prison Department in England and Wales*, 1977: Paragraph 152.

[14]*Report of the Work of the Prison Department in England and Wales*, 1979: Paragraph 110.

commercial production of crops and livestock, and about 1,500 acres are devoted to amenity grounds and sports areas'.[15]

Farming is the most profitable part of prison work, making an overall profit of £2,570,760 in 1979.[16] Most of the produce is sold to the prison department, and farming is generally associated with the low-security establishments, particularly open prisons.

The Works Department is responsible for the 'maintenance and improvement of existing premises and for the provision of new buildings'.[17] It employed 1195 men in 1979. Using prisoners to build more prisons is a cheaper way of constructing them. The Detention Centre at Eastwood Park, Gloucestershire, for example, was built almost entirely by prisoners from Leyhill and Bristol prisons. The men were transported daily to the site. 'This project is estimated to have cost twenty-five per cent less than an outside contract would have involved – a saving of about £100,000.'[18] Prisoners at Highpoint prison in Suffolk are currently employed in building a new maximum security prison.

'Domestic duties' include cleaning, kitchen, hospital and reception orderly work, and employed 6,135 men in 1979.[19] Much of this work is dull, soul-destroying, and labour-intensive. Modern cleaning equipment is a rare sight in prison, with the mop and brush being the most used implements. In 1979, 163 men were employed outside the prisons working during the day, and returning to the prison at night.[20] Many of them were involved in pre-release hostel schemes, which, as the numbers involved indicate, are rarely available in England and Wales. Men working full-time outside hand over their wages to the prison department, and receive only minimal payment.

The number involved in full-time education, including vocational and trade training, was 1,559 in 1979.[21] Given the aims of prison

---

[15]*Prisons and the Prisoner*, 1977: Paragraph 98.
[16]*Report of the Work of the Prison Department in England and Wales*, 1979: Paragraph 115.
[17]*Prisons and the Prisoner*, 1977: Paragraph 99.
[18]ibid.: Paragraph 100.
[19]*Prison Statistics, England and Wales*, 1979: Table 10.5.
[20]ibid.
[21]ibid.

work, and the total number of prisoners, this is a remarkably low figure. It indicates the gap between the dull monotony of prison labour and the official encouragement of 'the habit of regular and purposeful work at a tempo and in conditions as close as possible to those of outside industry'.[22]

In Scotland, prison work has not been re-organized into an organization such as Prindus, but similar types of work are undertaken. In 1979, 1,553 people were involved in manufacturing and productive work. Within manufacturing, the biggest group of prisoners (482) were employed in 'textiles', including sewing mailbags, kitbags, tailoring and protective clothing. Only four prisoners were engaged in farming work. The Works Department employed 112 prisoners working in the prisons as general labourers, painters and plumbers. 'Domestic duties' attracted the second largest group (660), and twenty-seven prisoners were engaged in full-time industrial training. As in England and Wales, trade training sometimes lasts only a matter of weeks, and, on completing the course, an individual might find himself allocated to a job where his newly acquired skill is redundant.[23] A pre-release hostel scheme operates at three prisons, but involves only about twenty prisoners.

It is not only the nature of the work and the conditions under which prisoners work which creates such a large gap between official policy and actual practice. It is also the wages prisoners receive. In 1979, prisoners earnings accounted for only four per cent of the gross expenditure on employment (England and Wales). Average earnings in 1979 were about £1.31 pence per week, with a maximum of over £2. In Scotland, in 1980, prisoners could earn up to £2.20 a week, but the majority earned well below that, often as little as 71 pence. However, *Prisons and the Prisoner* still felt able to argue that 'earnings do provide some incentive to work. They also provide the offender with some rewards for his efforts and some opportunity to have spending money and to think about how to spend it'.[24] It also argued that the days of prison work being punitive are over. But to prisoners sewing mailbags, stripping cables, making nuclear fall-out jackets, assembling components for aerosol sprays, dismantling

---

[22]*Prisons and the Prisoner*, 1977: Paragraph 90.
[23]*Prisons in Scotland*, 1979: Appendix 18.
[24]*Prisons and the Prisoner*, 1977: Paragraph 105.

telephone equipment, ripping up rags, cleaning the landings, painting the walls, and picking up excrement from under cell windows, work appears punitive.

Refusal to work is also punished, and if an individual's productivity is not up to standard, he can be disciplined. At Hull, for example, in 1976, prisoners had to earn 42 pence in a thirty hour week, working on outside contract work to qualify for a cost of living allowance. If they earned substantially less, they were put on report. On the third and any subsequent report, they lost remission.[25]

With their earnings, prisoners can buy extra letters, tea, sugar, milk, sweets, tobacco, matches (at full price), and have to contribute to TV and film rentals. In most prisons, they must also contribute to a 'common fund' for the buying and upkeep of recreational facilities. Earnings are not paid in cash, and no money officially circulates in prison. Each prisoner has an account to which prison earnings are added, and from which canteen purchases are deducted.

For British prisoners, then, the nature and conditions of work and the wages paid do not serve to enhance their own self-image, and can hardly be said to lead them to the good and useful life espoused by the prison department. Rather it suggests that people have been sent to prison not only *as* but also *for* punishment.

EDUCATION

Education in prisons has been described as 'a tool for a job, an aid to living and a contribution to the quality of life there'[26], and it has been acknowledged that 'there has always been a place for education in custodial treatment and training.'[27] Education has been a statutory requirement in prisons since 1823, but in adult prisons, where participation is voluntary, education has traditionally been a low priority, and continues to account for a tiny proportion of the total prison budget. In 1979, for example, education training and recreation accounted for £3,471,000 in a total expenditure of £206,731,000, in England and Wales. By contrast, expenditure on

---

[25]*Hull 1976*, 1977, 3.
[26]*Prisons and the Prisoner*, 1977: Paragraph 50.
[27]*Prisons and other penal establishments in Scotland*, 1978, 4.

travelling, removals and training of staff was £5,123,000.[28] In Scotland, of the overall net expenditure of £19,641,000 only £152,000 was allocated for education and recreation, compared with £362,000 on officers' travelling and removal expenses.[29] In England and Wales education is organized by the prison department with the support of Local Education Authorities. The LEAs provide the education officers, who are responsible for the overall organization of education within the prison. Most of the teaching is done by part-time teachers in the evenings. In 1977, educational services were provided by forty-nine LEAs, working through 118 education officers, forty-three deputies, 178 full-time teachers and 2,955 part-time teachers.[30] In Scotland, in 1979, there were eight education officers, seventeen full-time teachers, and six prison officer teachers, with some part-time teachers involved in day-time teaching.[31]

Throughout the prison system as a whole, a wide range of courses are offered, from remedial and literacy classes, to degree work with the Open University (OU) and university extra-mural departments. Vocational classes cover a variety of subjects, from navigation to 'current affairs'. But both facilities and the range of courses vary greatly from prison to prison, and within prisons over time. While the education officer organizes the provision of classes in a particular prison, it is the governor who has the ultimate responsibility for education, being able to decide without giving any explanation, whether or not particular courses will be offered, and which prisoners will be entitled to enrol for them.

The organization and uses of education in prisons raise a number of important issues. Although the prison authorities are statutorily obliged to provide educational facilities, education is a privilege, not a right for prisoners. A prisoner wishing to take a class must apply for permission to the governor. Books also have to be approved by individual prisons, often by the prison medical officer or chaplain. A course or book permitted in one prison is not necessarily allowed in

---

[28]*Report of the Work of the Prison Department in England and Wales*, 1979: Appendix 4.
[29]*Prisons in Scotland*, 1979: Appendix 21.
[30]*Report of the Work of the Prison Department in England and Wales*, 1977: Paragraph 41.
[31]*Prisons in Scotland*, 1979: Paragraph 51.

another. For the prisoner who is transferred during a course of study, this can cause serious difficulty, and even mean curtailment of education privileges.

Education has become an important part of the control system in prisons, and increasingly is designed to suit management rather than prisoners' purposes:

> Education not only relieves boredom but provides a means of acquiring knowledge or skills which will assist an offender who is so minded to live through his sentence sensibly, thereby being also of value to staff in the control and management situation . . .[32]

The provison of education is firmly embedded in the concern for control and security. In 1972, for example, following a summer of disturbances in the prisons, the *Report of the Work of the Prison Department* commented, 'the summer disturbances disrupted the prison education programme in some prisons – a practical illustration of good order and discipline being an essential basis for training.'[33] Again, in discussing the merits of the prison department's relationship with the Open University (111 prisoners in England and Wales sat for courses with the OU in 1979), *Prisons and the Prisoner* acknowledges that these studies 'have been valuable in taxing the wits of people who might otherwise have drifted through their sentences – at best, quiescent, perhaps unnoticed; at worst in trouble. Most have contributed to the stability in their establishments . . .'[34] The same importance attached to education as a means of keeping the lid on prisons was evident in the 1971 Report which concluded that education 'made a useful contribution to preserving the quality of life in those establishments where conditions continued to be difficult because of severe overcrowding.'[35] This official view is borne out by the experiences of the education officer at Lincoln prison: 'the

---

[32]*Prisons and the Prisoner*, 1977: Paragraph 50.
[33]*Report of the Work of the Prison Department in England and Wales*, 1972: Paragraph 57.
[34]*Prisons and the Prisoner*, 1977: Paragraph 52.
[35]*Report of the Work of the Prison Department in England and Wales*, 1971: Paragraph 55.

education that we have or that which comes under the heading of education is simply designed to usefully fill in time for those men with us; and it is confined to evening classes with some day classes for the people who can't read or write.'[36]

For the individual prisoner, trying to follow a course can be a difficult and harassing experience. The example of John Nightingale highlights the problems in the uses of education by the prison authorities. John Nightingale first registered to study for a degree with the Open University in 1977, taking the Social Sciences foundation course at Parkhurst prison:

> In September, a few weeks before the examination, he was transferred to Wandsworth, and all his course material was confiscated. Later, it was explained that he was 'suspected of taking part in subversive activities'. He was refused permission to sit the examination, and held in solitary confinement. At the end of October, the course material was suddenly returned, and he was told to prepare himself for a special exam in mid-November. During this time, he was denied access to tutorials and broadcasts, important components of OU courses. Despite this harassment, John passed the course.
>
> For his second year, he had registered to study the new 'Social Work, Community Work and Society' course. In early December 1977, he was told he would be allowed access to Course materials, but would not be allowed to submit any written work for assessment. Given that the OU is based partly on continual assessment, and partly on exams, this effectively prohibited him from working towards a degree.
>
> Following pressure on the Home Office, John was eventually moved from Wandsworth to Chelmsford, one of twenty-four prisons with OU facilities. He was allowed to begin the course. After a fire at Chelmsford, he was sent to Strangeways in Manchester, without his course material. Despite repeated requests, he was unable to find out if he would be allowed to continue his studies. In the meantime, he fell further behind with the continual assessment.
>
> The OU Regional Office in Manchester tried to arrange to see

---

[36]BBC Radio, *The Prisoners,* 'The Local Prison', 22 December 1977.

him, and sort out tutorials. Manchester is not on the list of prisons which offer OU courses. The course fees were due, and the Home Office initially refused to pay them, though later it did. Only then was John officially recognized as an OU student.

At Strangeways, John lived and worked in a cell with two other people, and was allowed no extra facilities for studying. The one tutorial which he was finally allowed was conducted in the presence of a prison officer.

In June, he was transferred again, to Maidstone, which has a reputation as a 'good' nick for studying and the educational welfare department there is comparatively well organized. John settled down to get on with the course. He was allowed to register for full-time study. In September, he was taken off full-time study, again a few weeks before the exam and told to go to work assembling plastic coat hangers. He refused and lost seven days remission.[37]

John Nightingale's case illustrates the contradictions inherent in prison education. On the one hand he, and others, have benefited from the courses they have taken. Particularly for long-termers, education can provide a means of getting through the sentence, and avoiding some of the most debilitating features of imprisonment.

On the other hand, these benefits have to be offset against difficulties faced by prisoners in some institutions. The most serious, and consistent, is that education is a privilege which can be withdrawn – without appeal. The situation in which a person begins a course of study can be drastically altered at the whim of individual prison governors. It is up to the prisoner to keep out of trouble, to avoid being punished by a discretionary decision sometimes taken to appease prison officers. In the *Abstract of the Rules and Regulations for Convicted Prisoners (Scotland)*, prisoners are explicitly warned that attendance at education classes 'is a privilege and subject to good behaviour'.[38]

Such difficulties are experienced not only by prisoners. People who teach in prison, either on a full-time or part-time basis, have to

---

[37] *The Leveller,* December 1978.
[38] *Abstract of the Rules and Regulations for Convicted Prisoners (Scotland):* Paragraph 22.

struggle to balance educational interests with the managerial imperatives of control and security. *The Handbook for Teachers* published by the Home Office illustrates the problems facing teachers, assuring them that 'personal relationships between teachers coming in from the free world and people in custody are just as important, perhaps even more important, than the subject which they both have under study, being, as it were, the point where attitudes are formed and reformed.'[39] On the other hand, paragraph 10 of the Handbook warns teachers against becoming too involved with prisoners' problems:

> People in custody sometimes try to interest teaching staff in their offences, sentences, regimes, supervisory staff, personal or family problems, fellow people in custody, grievances or complaints, in short anything to do with themselves during their custody. Nor is it unknown for them to try to persuade teaching staff to intercede with them for the courts, lawyers, Ministers of the Crown, Members of Parliament, or other prominent personages. It is no business of teaching staff to enter into discussion of such matters. There is other provision for ventilating them and this must be used. Teaching staff should report to the Tutor Organizer any attempts which are made to inveigle them into matters of this kind, and then take no further action. The Tutor Organizer will be responsible for whatever further action may be necessary.[40]

Like prisoners, teachers have to be seen to adhere to these commands. Pressure is brought to bear on those who are thought to waver. For example, teachers known to have built up good relationships with prisoners, have reported that they have arrived at prisons to find that no prison officer is available to escort them to the classroom. Prisoners were not informed that the teacher was actually waiting at the gatehouse, and classes were cancelled. New teachers are often given an introductory talk by the chief security officer, to emphasize the security and control aspects of education.

Prison officers are frequently posted outside, or even inside, the

---

[39] Cited in Cohen and Taylor, 1978, 78.
[40] ibid., 79.

classrooms, and the threat of an end to classes is as thinly veiled for teachers identified as 'troublesome' as it is for 'troublesome' prisoners.

Education facilities are well publicized outside the walls by the prison department. But this publicity ignores the major difficulties and obstacles which individual prisons place in the path of both the teachers and the taught. Education as a tool for living is also a weapon for control in the hands of the prison authorities.

LETTERS AND VISITS

Convicted prisoners have a right to send a letter on reception into prison, and one letter every week. Notepaper, envelope and postage are paid for from public funds. Around this bare statutory minimum has been developed a complex web of regulations, and privileges, woven together by discretion and censorship, which graphically illustrates the overall position of the imprisoned.

A prisoner is allowed to write to or receive letters from family, relatives and friends, although there are additional restrictions on Category A prisoners. (See page 46.) Extra - or canteen - letters may be purchased by prisoners from their weekly earnings, although these are a privilege which can be granted or refused at the discretion of the governor. In special circumstances, again determined by the governor, prisoners may be allowed to write an additional letter, paid from public funds. Every letter is headed with the surname and number of the prisoner, and the address of the prison. The only exception to this is where a parent is writing to a child under sixteen years old, or when the governor accepts that there are strong compassionate reasons for allowing plain paper.

Soon after reception, prisoners submit to the governor a list of people with whom they intend to correspond. The governor has discretionary powers to refuse permission to write to individuals on that list, and anybody not on the original list has to seek the governor's permission to correspond with a prisoner.

Every letter coming into, or going out from a prison is opened and read:

> Except as provided by these Rules, every letter or communication to or from a prisoner may be read or examined

by the governor or an officer deputed by him, and the governor may, at his discretion, stop any letter or communication on the ground that its contents are objectionable or of inordinate length.[41]

What is 'objectionable' and what is 'inordinate length' is nowhere agreed upon, but in practice is defined to fit in with the general situation both at a particular prison, and of the individual prisoners. The Standing Orders give a more detailed exposition of what is, and is not permissible. Ostensibly the reason for censorship of letters is security – the need to prevent forbidden articles being smuggled into the prison, or an escape plot being hatched – but in practice 'objectionable' has a much wider meaning.[42]

In November 1981, the Home Office announced changes in the secret rules governing the censorship of prisoners' mail. The revised rules abolished eight categories of material which prisoners were previously prevented from writing about. These categories include general complaints about prison conditions, statements about the courts, police and prison authorities, references to people in public life, and attempts to 'stimulate public agitation'. The rules were re-written to meet criticism from the European Commission of Human Rights which at the time was considering complaints from six prisoners. The Commission had found against Britain on the point that British prisoners had no effective channels for their grievances. The impact of the changes to the rules surrounding letter-writing have yet to be seen.

A prisoner who offends against any of the rules will be given back the letter with one opportunity to rewrite it. If the rewritten letter does not meet with the censor's approval, the letter will be forfeited.

Rule 33(3) and the related Standing Orders also apply to incoming mail. Offensive sections of letters written to a prisoner will either be deleted, or if the offending material is too long, the letter will be returned to the correspondent with a request to rewrite it.

In all, there are over 500 separate instructions dealing with communications alone, including the Prison Rules agreed by Parliament, and the Standing Orders which are administratively

---

[41] *Prison Rules, England and Wales,* 1964: Rule 33(3).
[42] See Cohen and Taylor, 1978, 52-3.

decreed, and amended and elaborated in an endless series of circular instructions. Most of these are classified as official secrets, and thus neither prisoners, nor outsiders writing to prisoners, can have access to, or even knowledge of them.

In practice, then, it is impossible to know in advance whether letters will contravene prison regulations, and thus be censored. On top of this, extra letters which are privileges, are used for disciplinary purposes. Thus Prison Rule 74(3) in Scotland states:

> When a prisoner who becomes entitled to write a letter, or receive a visit, is at the time subject to confinement to cell, the writing of the letter or the receipt of the visit may, in the governor's discretion, be deferred until the period of such confinement has expired, but not so as to extend the interval between letters or visits beyond eight weeks.[43]

Again, in the *Abstract of the Rules and Regulations for Convicted Prisoners* (Scotland), paragraph 23 emphasizes that letters are 'privileges which may be forfeited as a punishment'.[44]

The number of letters sent and received is also subject to the actions of the prison officers. In recent disruptive action by officers, letters to and from prisoners were witheld, because no member of staff was available to censor them. In local prisons, it is now standard practice that short-term prisoners are allowed to send out, and receive only one extra canteen letter a week (two for long-termers).

The censorship of content is one key element in the control of correspondence. The other involves the actual correspondents:

> Prisoners who conform to the general rules about what may be included in their letters are officially entitled to correspond with (and be visited by) close relations. This is strictly defined as husband and wife (including common-law husband or wife), parent, child, brother or sister. They will normally also be allowed to correspond with (and be visited by) other relatives and existing friends – but the governor may forbid this on the nebulous grounds of 'security or good order and discipline'. Finally, they may correspond with people not known to them

[43]*Prison Rules, Scotland,* 1952: Paragraph 74(3)
[44]*Abstract of the Prison Rules and Regulations for Convicted Prisoners (Scotland):* Paragraph 23.

before they came into custody only with the governor's permission (or as it is more severely stated in the Rules which are technically, if not actually, available to prisoners, 'with the leave of the Secretary of State').[45]

As Cohen and Taylor conclude, this set of restrictions upon what is written, and to whom, places a 'most formidable barrier between the prisoner and the outside world'.[46]

Visiting arrangements are similarly enmeshed in a massive number of regulations and circular instructions, most of which are secret. Statutorily, a convicted prisoner is entitled to one visit after sentence, and then one visit a month. In practice, as with letters, the number, length and conditions of visits vary from institution to institution. Prisoners at some institutions may receive fortnightly visits of up to one hour, while at another prison, the monthly visit may be restricted to twenty minutes. Even where visits are available fortnightly, not all visitors can afford them. Supplementary Benefits provides only for one visit a month, which means that only the better-off can afford the second 'privilege' visit. Additional visits may be granted in exceptional circumstances, or a prisoner may be allowed to accumulate visits, both at the discretion of the governor.

Visits may be made by a prisoner's family or friends, with the permission of the governor. All visits officially take place in the sight and hearing of a prison officer. In some prisons, a room with separate tables and chairs and light refreshments is laid on, but in others, visits can take place in the traditional visiting box 'with the prisoner sitting in one half and the visitor in the other, the two separated by glass and a wire grille'.[47] Another arrangement is 'to seat a number of prisoners along one side of a long table and the visitors along the other, and a supervising officer at the end'.[48] Prisoners are permitted to embrace visitors briefly only at the beginning and end of the visits. Prisoners are usually searched going to and from a visit. In some establishments children are allowed to sit on a prisoner's lap, but only with permission.

---

[45]Cohen and Taylor, 1978, 54.
[46]ibid.
[47]*Prisons and the Prisoner*, 1977: Paragraph 68.
[48]ibid.

Visitors must bring the Visiting Order (VO) sent by the prisoner, and hand it to the gate officers. Only those named on the VO will be allowed in. Not more than three people (excluding children) are allowed to visit at any one time. Many visitors have to travel considerable distances, at much expense, and there are few facilities provided for waiting, or for children. This is particularly true of isolated prisons, such as Dartmoor and Peterhead. To reach Peterhead from Glasgow, a prisoner's visitor has to make a three-hour train journey to Aberdeen, and an hour's bus journey from Aberdeen to Peterhead. With the waiting, the visit, and the return journey, often made at the weekend, when travel by public transport is particularly difficult, a single visit can take over twelve hours.

It is common to see a straggle of people standing outside many prison gates, in all weathers, waiting for their visit. Once inside, visitors are escorted at all times by prison staff. Visits take place in crowded conditions, with up to sixty other sets of visitors in the same area. Within the prison walls, visitors complain about dirty waiting rooms, poor, or non-existent facilities for children, inadequate sanitary provisions, and the lack of privacy to discuss intimate personal details:

> I've been to Wormwood Scrubs and that's a sore subject. It really is bad. There is nothing there, the kids can't even play. There might have been heating but I didn't see any and if you want to go to the toilet, there is only one. You have to wait outside in the corridor where everyone can see you.
>
> Wakefield is better, there is a room for the kids with a roundabout and toys and they have a woman to look after them. I wouldn't say that it's nice, but it's the best I've seen so far.
>
> I get there about 12.30 and the big wooden doors open and I go into the waiting room. There are warders all around the room, two or three sitting at a table and one on the door, but you don't usually get a table near them. It is as private as you can get, but you can't really show any affection. I don't even write affectionate letters, as I know that other people are going to read them.[49]

---

[49] *Community Care*, 2 November 1977, 4.

As Cohen and Taylor demonstrate:

> what seems to have happened – as in so many other areas of prison life – is that a reasonable concern for security has been magnified in such a way as to justify a whole range of checks and counter-checks which effectively deprive the prisoner of any freedom to write what he wishes, to whomever he wishes, and to be regularly visited by people of his own choice.[50]

For many prisoners, and their families and friends the stresses and strains of maintaining close contact become too great, and the obstacles placed in their way by the prison authorities become insurmountable. Ultimately, prisoners lose contact with the world outside the prison, which makes their eventual return even more difficult. It is hard to reconcile this situation with the prison authorities' public concern to 'emphasize the importance both of helping the prisoner to see himself as a member of society and preserving his vital links with his wife and family'.[51]

DISCIPLINE

The concept of 'good order and discipline' is the central and overriding tenet of the prison system, and can, when it is threatened, lead to the postponement or suspension of other features of prison life, for example, letters, visits, education, and welfare. The consequences of the increasing security-consciousness of the prison authorities and staff are discussed in the next chapter. Here we are concerned with the nature of offences against 'good order and discipline', the adjudication proceedings, the types of punishments ('awards') handed out, as they affect the individual prisoner, and prisoners' complaints procedures.

As in other areas of prison life, one of the consequences of the secrecy which surrounds imprisonment is that prisoners are not allowed access to the rules and regulations which they are supposed to keep. On entering a cell for the first time, prisoners are supposed to be given a copy of *General Notes for the Guidance of Convicted*

---

[50]Cohen and Taylor, 1978, 49.
[51]*Prisons and the Prisoner*, 1977: Paragraph 65.

Prisoners (in England and Wales), or the *Abstract of the Rules and Regulations for Convicted Prisoners (Scotland)*. These are summaries of those parts of the prison rules and regulations which the prison authorities have decided prisoners should know about. The summaries provide no more than the briefest guide, and omit or conceal all sorts of other rules and provisions; for example there is no reference to Rule 33(3) on the censorship of prison letters. A prisoner is frequently not allowed to see a full copy of the Prison Rules, and has no right of access to the Standing Orders, Circular Instructions, and Governor's Handbook. What is more, these rules cannot be challenged in the outside courts, as they 'have no formal legal status in the sense of falling under the jurisdiction of the English (and Scottish) legal system.'[52] Prison rules then, and the administration of justice in the prisons are substantially beyond the law.

The Governor's Handbook, Standing Orders, Circular Instructions, and the official Prison Rules, are so comprehensive that it is hard to imagine any aspect of prison life which is not covered down to the smallest detail by some regulation or another.

Prison Rule 47 (in Scotland, Prison Rule 42) covers most of the incidents liable to threaten good order and discipline.

A prisoner shall be guilty of an offence against discipline if he:

1 mutinies or incites another prisoner to mutiny;
2 does gross personal violence to an officer;
3 does gross personal violence to any person not being an officer;
4 commits any assault;
5 escapes from prison or from legal custody;
6 absents himself without permission from any place where he is required to be, whether within or outside prison;
7 has in his cell or room or in his possession any unauthorized article, or attempts to obtain such an article;
8 delivers or receives from any person, without permission, anything he is allowed to have only for his own use;
9 sells or delivers to any other person, without permission, anything he is allowed to have only for his own use;

---

[52]Cited in Cohen and Taylor, 1978, 24.

10 takes improperly or is in unauthorized possession of any article belonging to another person or to a prison;

11 wilfully damages or disfigures any part of the prison or any property not his own;

12 makes any false and malicious allegation against an officer;

13 treats with disrespect an officer or any person visiting a prison;

14 uses any abusive, insolent, threatening or other improper language;

15 is indecent in language, act or gesture;

16 repeatedly makes groundless complaints;

17 is idle, careless or negligent at work, or being required to work, refuses to do so;

18 disobeys any lawful order or refuses or neglects to conform to any rule or regulation of the prison;

19 attempts to do any of the foregoing things;

20 in any way offends against good order and discipline; or

21 does not return to prison when he should have returned after being temporarily released from prison under Rule 6 of these rules, or does not comply with any condition upon which he was released.[53]

Prison Rule 42 in Scotland is similarly all-embracing.

Prisoners who are seen to have broken one or more of these rules are put 'on report' by a prison officer. An officer does not have to inform prisoners that they are being put on report. Every prisoner is notified with a 'Notice to Inmate' (Form 1127), with details of the sections of Rule 47 contravened. As soon as a prisoner is put on report he can be segregated and put in solitary confinement until the case is heard. Prisoners are supposed to sign Form 1127 to verify that they have received the charge and can, if they wish, write out a defence statement, and name people they want to call as witnesses. Justice in prisons is summary. Statutorily, prisoners are only entitled to two hours notice of the impending disciplinary proceedings in which to prepare their defence.

Offences against Prison Rule 47 are dealt with either by the governor or the Board of Visitors. The governor (or his deputy or

---

[53]*Prison Rules, England and Wales*, 1964: Rule 47.

assistant) deals with minor charges, usually on the morning following the offence.

The prisoner is searched and then escorted into the 'orderly room' in the prison wing. The governor is seated behind a table, and the chief officer stands to the right of the governor. Other prison officers may be present. The prisoner stands to attention, three feet in front of the governor. In some prisons, two officers stand at the shoulders of the prisoner, facing him. The prisoner is asked by the chief officer for his name, number and length of sentence. The charges are then read out. The officer making the report describes what has happened. The prisoner is then given an opportunity to make any comments or to ask questions. He cannot address the accusing officer directly, but must ask his questions through the governor. The governor can judge the prisoner's questions to be irrelevant or impertinent, and therefore not ask them. The prisoner can call witnesses only with the approval of the governor. Many prisoners will not appear as witnesses for fear of being charged with making 'false and malicious allegations against a prison officer'. Prisoners may then make a statement in mitigation before punishment is 'awarded'. Governors can 'award' any one, or a combination of the following punishments:

(a) Caution;
(b) Forfeiture for a period not exceeding twenty-eight days (fourteen days in Scotland) of any of the privileges under Rule 4 of these Rules;
(c) Exclusion from associated work for a period not exceeding fourteen days;
(d) Stoppage of earnings for a period not exceeding twenty-eight days;
(e) Cellular confinement for a period not exceeding three days;
(f) Forfeiture for any period in the case of a prisoner otherwise entitled thereto who is guilty of escaping or attempting to escape, of the right to wear clothing of his own under Rule 20(i) of these Rules.[54] [Such prisoners are usually required to wear distinctive patched clothing.]

If prisoners are to be sentenced to solitary confinement, they will

---

[54]Cited in Cohen and Taylor, 1978, 30.

be examined by a medical officer to ensure that they are fit to serve the sentence. There is no right of appeal, and sentences are carried out immediately.

Prisoners charged with more serious offences, such as mutiny, incitement to riot, gross personal violence, assaulting a prison officer, escaping, or with persistent previous offences are dealt with by the Board of Visitors. It can impose much more severe penalties.

In 1979, less than seven per cent of adjudications in male prisons in England and Wales were made by the Board of Visitors.[55] Officially, the Board of Visitors has three main functions:

(a) they constitute an independent body of representatives of the local community to which any inmate may make a complaint or request, both at their regular meetings (usually held at intervals of a few weeks) and during the visits which individual members make between meetings;

(b) their members regularly visit and inspect all parts of the establishment, paying particular reference to the state of the premises, the quality of the administration as it affects inmates, and the treatment – in its widest senses – which inmates receive, with a view to reporting and making recommendations to the Home Secretary on any incompetence or abuse which may come to their notice;

(c) as the superior disciplinary authority of the establishment, they adjudicate when inmates are charged with any of the relatively serious offences against discipline.[56]

As it is both a disciplinary body, and a receiver of prisoners' complaints, the Board is supposed to be independent of the prison and to have an 'uncommitted point of view'.[57] Quite how independent can be seen from the membership of the Board. All members are local dignitaries, usually from the professional classes, appointed by the Home Office. The Home Secretary is responsible for appointing the first Chairman, and names of other members are usually submitted to the Home Office via the governor and local

---

[55]*Prison Statistics England and Wales*, 1979: Table 9(a).
[56]*Prisons and the Prisoner*, 1977: Paragraph 59.
[57]ibid: Paragraph 61.

chairman. In 1975, nearly two-thirds of the 1,400 members of BOVs were more than fifty years old, and nearly sixty per cent were lay-magistrates. At any one sitting, not more than five and at least two members of the Board must be present; 'where the alleged offence is mutiny, incitement to mutiny or gross personal violence to an officer, the minimum is three members, and at least two must be magistrates.'[58]

A minimum of two hours notice must be given to the person appearing before the Board, and he or she should be medically examined. The Board is not supposed to have access to previous disciplinary charges against an individual before the hearing. The 'court' procedure is the same as the governor's hearing. Prisoners may call witnesses, but only with the consent of the chairman of the Board, and questions to witnesses must be directed through the chairman. The prisoner is taken out of the room while the Board considers its verdict. The governor is present throughout the proceedings, but should leave the room before the prisoner. If found guilty, the prisoner will be given an opportunity to present any mitigating circumstances, and, as at the governor's hearing, will be able to call any person who is 'readily available' to support him or her. The governor will then inform the Board of the prisoner's general conduct in the prison and any previous disciplinary record. The Board will then impose sentence, making one or more of the following awards:

(a) caution;
(b) forfeiture for any period of any of the privileges under Rule 4 of these Rules;
(c) exclusion from associated work for a period not exceeding fifty-six days;
(d) stoppage of earnings for a period not exceeding fifty-six days;
(e) cellular confinement for a period not exceeding fifty-six days;
(f) forfeiture of remission of a period not exceeding 180 days. (No limit of time in Scotland.)

---

[58]ibid: Paragraph 86.

Forfeiture of remission in excess of 180 days may be made for the following offences:

(a) mutiny or incitement to mutiny;
(b) doing gross personal violence to an officer.[59]

Since 1978, following a High Court action, prisoners in England and Wales now have the right to appeal to outside courts against sentences imposed by the Boards of Visitors. (We discuss this in detail in chapter 6.)

Throughout any disciplinary proceedings, prisoners have no *right* to call witnesses, to cross-examine the prosecuting officer, to have any legal help, to appeal against the verdict of the sentence. It is also clear that the Boards of Visitors are not the independent body the prison department claim they are. The Jellicoe review of the Boards concluded cautiously:

> Generally speaking all the ex-prisoners who wrote to us, and some of the most thoughtful individual Board members, felt that the system was loaded against the inmate.[60]

The Board of Visitors is not only concerned with prison discipline. As we have seen, they also hear the complaints of prisoners, and oversee general prison conditions. As the Chairman of the Board of Visitors at Maidstone prison observed:

> We are an independent body, appointed by the Home Secretary to be the eyes and ears of the public. Our role is to act as independent observers and to concern ourselves with the prison as a whole – both the officers and the inmates. It is laid down that we must visit the prison twice a month, and interest ourselves in such things as the quality and standard of food, the work, recreation, etc. It is also possible for a man to see any one of us privately, by applying to do so.[61]

---

[59]Cited in Cohen and Taylor, 1978, 35.
[60]*Boards of Visitors of Penal Institutions*, 1975, 37.
[61]*Inside Out*, September 1978, Edition 6, H.M. Prison Maidstone.

But, in practice, the Boards of Visitors are very much part of the institutional apparatus of control in prisons, either by directly disciplining prisoners, or by serving as a filter through which all complaints must pass. To make a complaint to the BOV, a prisoner must receive permission from the governor. The primary aim of the Board of Visitors must be to maintain good order and discipline in the institutions. In a situation where the evidence is usually the prisoner's word versus the prison officer's, Boards will generally favour the latter.

As the Chairman of the Board of Visitors at Lincoln Prison commented:

> It's very difficult. If we're convinced that the prisoner is not guilty, we'll find the prisoner not guilty. If it's a bit of a toss up or we're fairly convinced he did it but there isn't necessarily a legal proof, possibly hearsay, something of that sort, we, as likely as not, for the good of the establishment, would support the officer.[62]

Not all offences against the prison rules are dealt with by the governor or the Board of Visitors. Minor incidents will often be ignored or dealt with summarily by the prison officer concerned, and there is an array of informal 'punishments' which can be imposed. Regular reports about prisoners are made by officers and 'troublesome' prisoners may well find themselves moved from a single to a two or three'd up cell, from a preferred to a less attractive and 'well-paid' job, or that educational or recreational facilities are suddenly limited. Transferring prisoners from one prison to another is a further informal method of punishment. Physical brutality is also well known.

Another device is the use of 'cellular confinement', or Rule 43 (Rule 36 in Scotland). Rule 43 permits a governor to segregate a prisoner for up to twenty-eight days in the interests of 'good order and discipline'. This may be renewed indefinitely. A member of the Board of Visitors is required to approve the decision within twenty-four hours, but his authorization can be made retrospectively or by

---

[62]BBC Radio *The Prisoners,* 'The Local Prison', 22 December 1977.

telephone. Rule 43 is best known for voluntary segregation of particular prisoners or categories of prisoner (for example, sex offenders and informers) who would be at risk in the general prison population. But it is also used as a form of punishment without recourse to a charge being levelled and 'proved'. Again, there is no appeal against cellular confinement.

Given this situation, it is not surprising that prisoners have, with outside support, sought to challenge the legality of both the prison rules and the disciplinary procedures, through both British courts and the European Court for Human Rights in Strasbourg. These challenges, and the responses to them of the prison authorities are discussed in chapter 6.

As in the other aspects of imprisonment we have discussed, discretion, arbitrariness, expediency and unfairness are the hallmarks of discipline in British prisons.

MEDICAL PROVISION

The prison medical service has a general responsibility for the physical and mental health of all those in custody. Every penal institution has a hospital of some sort. In small institutions, the hospital will consist of a 'ward' (one or two single rooms), a treatment room and a consulting room. Larger prisons have more extensive facilities, and there are four prisons with surgical facilities in England and Wales, at Liverpool for the North, Wormwood Scrubs for the South, Parkhurst and Grendon Underwood. (There are no surgical facilities in Scottish prisons.) Medical officers are appointed to each establishment on a full or part-time basis. In Scotland, only Barlinnie has full-time medical officers. Part-timers are appointed from the local area in which the institution is situated, full-timers are members of the Prison Medical Service, an organization which is separate from the National Health Service (NHS). All are subject to the Official Secrets Act, even part-timers, who work under the auspices of the prison departments, and not the National Health Service.

Medical officers have wide-ranging and increasingly important duties and influence in the prisons, covering every aspect of imprisonment. At reception, for example, they are responsible for medically examining each individual prisoner, and, in the case of the convicted, deciding on their fitness to work. Doctors also compile medical reports on convicted prisoners remanded in custody to await sentence. In 1979, prisoners sought medical attention on 1,111,853 occasions, almost 50,000 more than in 1978. The number of admissions to prison hospitals for observation or treatment was 50,934, a thirty per cent increase from 1978.[63] Within the day-to-day running of all prisons, the medical officer is expected to advise on food, hygiene, working conditions, suitability of candidates for employment in the prison service, fitness of members of staff, accidents to and assaults on prisoners and staff, the fitness of prisoners for disciplinary 'awards', and prisoners who refuse food or who inflict self-injury, as well as overseeing the general physical and mental health of the prison population.

As successive prison department reports make clear, the Prison Medical Service makes considerable use of NHS facilities. In 1979, for example, prisoners attended out-patient departments of NHS hospitals on 14,770 occasions, and 1,299 prisoners were admitted to NHS hospitals for in-patient treatment in England and Wales. Medical officers also referred 89,267 prisoners to specialists and NHS consultants, and consultant psychiatrists visited prisons on 3,414 occassions to examine and prepare reports on prisoners at the request of their solicitors.[64]

Medical officers are assisted by hospital officers who are prison officers with a rudimentary nursing training. According to Standing Orders, the hospital officer in charge is responsible for the maintenance of proper order in the hospital and for ensuring the instructions of the governor and medical officer are carried out. Under the same Orders, provision is made for emergency situations when medical officers can give verbal instructions for the administration of controlled drugs, and has only to provide written instructions covering his verbal request within twenty-four hours after the event. Hospital officers are expected to carry out a wide range of duties within prison hospitals, despite having

---

[63]*Report of the Work of the Prison Department in England and Wales,* 1979: Paragraph 146.
[64]ibid: Paragraphs 145-7.

a training which, according to one officer, only 'scraped the surface of nursing in general'.[65]

The involvement of nursing officers in medical provision has been criticized by the Society of Radiographers. In 1977 the same Society was reported as being concerned that radiography was being undertaken in prisons by prison officers who do not possess the necessary training and qualifications which are statutory requirements in the NHS.[66]

Despite their dependence on NHS facilities, and support from part-time NHS doctors, the Prison Medical Service has resisted strenuously any attempt to incorporate it into the NHS. This has serious consequences for prisoners. Under the 1948 National Health Act, everyone has the right to choose his or her own doctor. But, under Prison Rule 17, prisoners have no choice, and must accept the prison medical officer as responsible for their health and well-being. Complaints about medical treatment or lack of it have to be directed to the governor or the Board of Visitors. There is no mechanism for outside independent scrutiny of medical care. Prison doctors are 'not responsible to, and hence cannot be censured by the Regional Health Authority, which has no power to investigate any complaints by prisoners. Community Health Councils similarly do not include prisoners in their terms of reference. Professional bodies such as the General Medical Council and the British Medical Association have shown a singular unreadiness to trespass on territory which the Home Office so zealously guards.'[67] Furthermore criticism of unsanitary conditions in prisons has been made according to the *Sunday Telegraph* by the Director of the North West Metropolitan Blood Transfusion Service.[68]

Outside security is important because of the medical officers' closeness to the prison officials. The demands and interests of 'good order and discipline' in the prisons frequently conflict with an individual prisoner's interests and health. A clear illustration of this is provided by the role of the prison doctor in passing people fit for work. It is a punishable offence to refuse to work unless certified

[65]*Prison Officers' Magazine*, August 1978.
[66]*Guardian*, 2 July 1977.
[67]Cohen and Taylor, 1978, 66.
[68]*Sunday Telegraph*, 26 August 1974.

unfit by the prison doctor, and prisoners lose a day's remission for each day they do not work. Prisoners constantly complain of being forced to work when they are ill. Prison doctors, on the other hand like other prison staff, complain of the 'malingering' of 'work-shy' prisoners.[69] It is not made clear to the prisoner when the doctor is acting in his interests, or when in the institution's interests. Nor is it made clear that doctors have this conflict of loyalties, and that information about their health, which would be strictly confidential on the outside, is available to the governor and other members of the prison staff, and used in making decisions about the conditions under which a person is held. Confidentiality is limited by the needs of the institution, to the point where many prisoners view the doctor as just another type of prison officer.

Prisoners also complain of the type of medical treatment they receive. Requests to see the doctor must be made after unlocking in the morning. Examinations are often brief and cursory, with prisoners given little time to explain their symptoms. Frequently, they do not see the doctor but only the nursing officer. As we have shown, nursing officers have only a rudimentary medical knowledge, and are hardly qualified to make decisions about the health of prisoners. Even when they see a doctor, prisoners frequently complain of medical maltreatment.

Indeed the increasing volume of complaints led the Home Office in the 1978 *Report of the Work of the Prison Department* to observe that 'the Prison Medical Service was the target for many inaccurate but apparently concerted attacks on its ethics and standards of treatment.'[70] It is very difficult to secure independent investigation and substantiation of prisoners' complaints about medical treatment. This increase may simply reflect greater willingness on the part of prisoners to try to take action against the prison authorities, rather than any increase in incidents of alleged medical malpractice. Although the Prison Department claims that it 'did its best' to respond to these criticisms, the Official Secrets Act and other all-too-familiar legal devices have made the task of discussing and verifying prisoners' allegations evermore hazardous. What seems

---

[69]Prewer, 1974.
[70]*Report of the Work of the Prison Department in England and Wales,* 1978: Paragraph 7.

quite clear, however, is that the Prison Department has misled and misinformed the public on these issues. To take but one example: the controversy over the use of drugs in prison. As we indicate elsewhere in this book, the Home Office had always given the impression that it knew exactly what drugs were dispensed and under what circumstances, but had not been prepared to divulge this information. Yet, in June 1979, it finally admitted that it had 'no check or monitor' on what drugs prison medical officers prescribe. Apart from a pilot experimental scheme in 1979, the Prison Department had not asked medical officers to tell them what drugs were used and for what reasons.

While it is frequently claimed that standards of medical care in prisons compare favourably with those of the National Health Service, general practitioners in the NHS have their prescribing patterns checked, and hospital doctors can be scrutinized by other doctors, the nursing staff and hospital pharmacist. But the prison medical officer has complete and unchecked clinical autonomy. A prison doctor simply writes instructions and drugs are handed out, often by a 'trained' prison officer.[71]

The Royal College of Psychiatrists, in its evidence to the May Inquiry, argued:

> Since prisoners are already disadvantaged, the facilities available for their treatment should be at least equal to those in the community. However, the high morbidity of those imprisoned, which can be compounded by disabilities induced by the process of imprisonment itself, is met by a general tendency to reject and scapegoat prisoners so that the services provided for them are often minimal.[72]

We would argue that a full independent investigation of prison medical facilities should be undertaken. Moreover, prisoners should have the right to consult with any doctor in the area in which they are imprisoned. In the long-term, we are concerned not only with the evidence of the increasing medicalization of problems in the prison system in particular, but throughout society as a whole. It should be

---

[71]*New Society,* 28 June 1979.
[72]*Bulletin of the Royal College of Psychiatrists,* May 1979, 83.

remembered that crucial questions and issues, such as the use of drugs, which are raised in a specific form inside penal institutions, are also of course central to the nature and extent of health care outside the prison walls.

WOMEN

At the end of 1979 the number of women imprisoned, while still small compared with the number of men, had reached its highest level in England and Wales since 1945. This was reflected not only in the average daily women prison population, but also in the total number of receptions.

The largest increase in the last three years has been in the number of women sentenced to short terms of imprisonment of six months or less.[73] For example, in 1976 the number of adult women sentenced to six months or less was fifty-four per cent of all those sentenced, in 1979 it had risen to sixty-two per cent.[74] The decision to open Cookham Wood, previously intended as a remand centre for young males, as a closed prison for women, indicates that the trend of sending more women to prison is to continue.

Women remanded in custody to await trial or sentence are housed at Holloway in London, Risley in Lancashire, Pucklechurch in Bristol, or Low Newton in Durham. The occassional Category A remands are kept at Brixton (a male prison), in conditions of strict solitary confinement.[75] In Scotland, women are remanded in the only women's prison, Cornton Vale, near Stirling, regardless of where they committed the alleged offence.

On conviction, women in England and Walers are sent immediately to either Holloway or Styal to be categorized and classified. Holloway was built in 1853, and first used exclusively for women in 1902. Since October 1970, the prison has been progressively demolished and rebuilt, and, at the end of 1977, had accommodation for 222. Overcrowding is severe: in 1977, the average daily population was 332, with a peak of 375.[76]

---

[73]*Prison Statistics England and Wales*, 1979, 55.
[74]ibid: Table 5(a).
[75]*Release*, 1978, 112-13.
[76]*Report of the Work of the Prison Department in England and Wales*, 1977: Appendix 3.

Eventually, Holloway, with accommodation for 500 women, will serve the south of England as a remand centre and local prison. It will also continue to have a national role, however, 'because it will consist basically of a secure hospital with medical, surgical and psychiatric facilities as its central feature.'[77] The idea that a women's prison should be a hospital illustrates the different conceptions of female and male offenders, which implies that while men are generally bad and in need of punishment, women are seen as 'sick' and in need of treatment, and the prison regimes differ accordingly.

The central aim of the prison authorities is to provide individualized treatment for women prisoners. Although establishments for women operate under the same rules as those for men, 'experience has shown that various specialist facilities are needed in dealing with women.' Great emphasis is placed on 'the continuity of personal relationships, on education and related training, and the constructive use of privileges', and the ratio of staff to prisoners is deliberately higher than in men's prisons.[78] The net result is that women's prisons, while apparently more relaxed than men's in that they have more privileges, can in fact be more oppressive. Women are denied self-determination: their crimes are seen as a 'cry for help', a sign of their mental illness or of their inadequacy, or as 'irrational, irresponsible and largely unintentional behaviour'.[79] According to the Prison Department, 'most of the women in prison wish to conform with society, but are unable to do so.'[80] As a (male) deputy governor at Styal observed, 'many women prisoners are neurotic and unstable. Perhaps all this is the result of a more permissive society, more liberal education, a lack of discipline and parental guidance.'[81]

The only exceptions to this general pattern are Category A women, now kept in a security wing of Durham prison, which specializes in receiving women serving long terms of imprisonment at the start of their sentences.[82] The regime at Durham is built around security

---

[77]*Prisons and the Prisoner*, 1977: Paragraph 181.
[78]ibid: Paragraph 178.
[79]Smart, 1977, 145.
[80]*Prisons and the Prisoner*, 1977: Paragraph 178.
[81]*Community Care*, 2 November 1977, 34.
[82]*Report of the Work of the Prison Department in England and Wales*, 1975: Paragraph 142.

considerations, and is effectively a 'prison within a prison'. At the corner of the L-shaped wing is a control box staffed at all times, which is so designed that officers can see out, but the women prisoners cannot see in. Cameras are trained on the women at all times, voice-pattern boxes have been installed at all points of entry to the wing and dogs are used to escort prisoners. Certain cells have bullet-proof glass, and all cell doors are electronically operated. At night, the doors can only be opened with the permission, and in the presence of, the governor or a deputy. Prisoners are not locked in their cells during the day, but it is an offence for more than three women to be in any cell at the same time.

Despite the differing official aims, women prisoners follow the same sort of daily routine as described for men. Work is limited, with the major emphasis, predictably, being on domestic and kitchen work, sewing and cleaning. Outside contract work is undertaken, and is of the most menial kind, for example, painting headlights on toy trucks, or assembling plastic toys. At Styal, women are frequently employed as machinists, making shirts, pyjamas and sports wear.

One major difference is in living accommodation. Women prisoners live in 'rooms' rather than cells. At Holloway, toilet facilities are built into each room. At Styal, women are housed in 'cottages' holding between eighteen and twenty-two people, except for long-termers who live in a separate house with a room for each prisoner.

We have remarked that women's prisons can be more oppressive than men's. Rules are more rigorously enforced, and the average number of disciplinary charges brought against women prisoners is consistently higher than the number brought against men. In 1977, an average of 3.02 charges were levelled against women, compared with 1.20 for men.[83] The extra privileges that women are allowed, for example, being able to wear their own clothes, are less a consequence of more liberal regimes for women, and rather because women are seen as less of a security risk. As *Prisons and the Prisoner* comments, 'there has been less public anxiety and fear when women have escaped from custody.'[84]

---

[83]*Prison Statistics in England and Wales*, 1977: Tables 9.2 and 9.3.
[84]*Prisons and the Prisoner*, 1977: Paragraph 178.

Even in the mother and baby units at Holloway (with places for eight) and Styal (with places for about fifteen), regimentation is the characteristic feature. Generally reserved for women who give birth while in prison, life in these units is as regulated for the babies as it is for the women. Mothers, for example, cannot decide feeding times, and no-one picks up the babies between feeds. There are no provisions for children in prison to be taken on outside visits. Children can live with their mothers at Holloway and Styal until they are twelve months old, and at Askham Grange open prison until two years.[85]

The rationale behind the mother and baby units also indicates the prison authorities' view of the place of women in the outside world:

To send a woman to prison, or indeed to any residential institution – even a hospital – is to take her away from her family; her children, in particular, may suffer from this deprivation, which can lead to the break-up of the home even where there is a stable marriage. When a man is absent from home, it can be kept going by his wife if she is provided with sufficient money and general support. But when it is the woman who is absent, the husband is often unable to cope and unless there are relations who can take on the housekeeping and care of the children, the home may have to be broken up and the children scattered, either into the care of the local authority, or to different relatives.[86]

It is this conception of the role of women, coupled with a particular explanation of their criminal behaviour, which explains not only the fact, but also the nature of women's imprisonment.

What has become clear in this analysis of the qualitative aspects of imprisonment is the extent to which secrecy, expediency, arbitrariness and discretion are the cornerstones of the British prison system. There are inumerable rules, regulations, standing orders and circular instructions used to buttress a pernicious system of privileges which can be both offered as inducements to good behaviour and

---

[85]*Release*, 1978, 113-14.
[86]*Prisons and the Prisoner*, 1977: Paragraph 185.

withdrawn as punishments for misbehaviour. This system of rules, regulations and privileges exists independently of the numbers of people imprisoned and the amount of overcrowding. A reduction of the prison population will not in itself relieve these conditions.

4 CONTAINMENT AND CONTROL

> By 1968, it had become clear that captivity was a central and problematic task in itself, requiring strategic planning and careful management. If anything else could be accomplished in the way of treatment and training, well and good . . .[1]

In the late 1960s and throughout the 1970s, the aspirations of Prison Rule 1 (5 in Scotland) were finally buried beneath burgeoning structures of control. The concern with containment not only subordinated but infiltrated other aims and ideas particularly those relating to 'treatment and training'. We have seen, for example, how education is designed to reinforce good order and discipline.

While the impact of containment is felt throughout the prison system, the justification for rigorous security and control is to be found not in the total prison population, but in a small minority of prisoners, variously categorized as 'troublemakers', 'subversives', 'people with nothing to lose', 'recalcitrants' and so on. This chapter explores the definition of, and responses to this minority which have been the excuse for a disproportionately large injection of resources, human and financial, to implement the policy of containment, and examines the consequences this has had for the prison system as a whole. This chapter revolves around three questions: who are these 'troublesome' prisoners; where and under what sorts of regime have they been contained;

---

[1]King and Elliott, 1977, 9.

and what practices have been adopted to make them conform to the rules and regulations of the prison system?

'ONE BAD APPLE'

The idea of classifying prisoners is not new. We have already noted that one of the first official expressions of the need to separate one type of prisoner from another can be found in the 1895 Gladstone Committee's report on imprisonment. Since then, the prison authorities have developed increasingly complex systems of grading designed to prevent not only the 'moral contamination' of one prisoner by another, but also to facilitate day to day organization of, and control over the imprisoned. Such systems are premised upon the belief that, while all prisoners are bad, some are worse than others and merit particular attention. Recently this idea has been refined to present an image of prisoners being divided into two groups. On the one hand, it is argued, there are the majority who recognize the legitimacy of their imprisonment, and of the prison authorities' methods of dealing with them, and simply want to serve their sentences quietly, and be released. On the other hand, there is a second small group, a 'hardcore', who, either unwilling or unable to settle down and serve their time, not only challenge the prison system but manipulate the first group to further their own ends. It is in this second group that the source of discontent and trouble in the prisons is seen to be located. This stereotyping of the imprisoned population has been made by prison staff, the prison department, Members of Parliament, and many outside commentators on penal affairs, and has become the framework in which the crisis of containment is defined and discussed.

In 1969, an article in the *Prison Officers' Magazine* outlined this position:

> Prisoners who would willingly serve their sentences with no intention of causing trouble, do so alongside those who lack whatever it takes to face up to the punishment for crime. But it is the irresponsible anarchical minority who stir up and incite the more reasonable element by threats, in some cases, to be parties to demonstrations and disturbances of varous sorts . . .

Troublemakers serving long sentences have seen their escape opportunities disappear with the introduction of the 'Mountbatten' reforms. As a result they are trying to enlist sympathy for themselves by fermenting trouble and blaming it on alleged inhuman restrictions, which are imposed by small-minded bullies in blue uniforms.[2]

These sentiments were reinforced in 1970 (and on frequent occasions since) by the General Secretary of the Prison Officers' Association, who in describing the crisis in prisons declared that the 'vast majority of prisoners ask no more than to be left alone to serve their sentence with the maximum amount of remission. We are talking about a small minority of men who are in prison for so long they do not care'.[3] At the same time, in his address to the annual conference, the Chairman of the POA, reflected that most prisoners were willing to serve their sentences, 'but there was a hardcore of sophisticated, dangerous psychopathic villains who make full use of the misguided and the inadequate to achieve their own evil ends.'[4]

The Home Secretary, in his 1973 address to the Boards of Visitors' Annual Conference in London, similarly argued that the 'increase in serious and violent crime means an increasing number of men, some of them relatively young, coming into our prisons to serve long sentences, and we must accept that this will continue to create serious problems in discipline and control.'[5] And in the full debate on the prison system in the House of Commons in 1977, Christopher Mayhew, addressing himself to the 'crisis of control' in prisons, warned:

There is a hard and extremely toxic core in the prison population that has nothing to lose. Its members cause immense disruption in any prison quite disproportionate to their numbers . . . Such prisoners do not lack – this is a modern manifestation – for powerful support outside, support that is vocal and well-organized in many cases.[6]

---

[2] *Prison Officers' Magazine*, 9 December 1969, 376.
[3] *The Times*, 5 August 1970.
[4] ibid., 20 May 1970.
[5] Home Secretary's Speech to the Board of Visitors, Press Release, 1973.
[6] *Hansard*, 18 March 1977: Column 773.

Beneath all these remarks lie a number of important, and generally unchallenged assumptions about where this minority came from, and how they have managed to focus attention on themselves. The increasing number of people serving long sentences is the most obvious source of 'troublemakers'. It is argued that since the abolition of capital punishment, prisons have had to cope with a 'new breed of prisoners with nothing to lose'.[7] Thus Peter Evans of *The Times* argued in 1976:

> The prisons now contain 106 people convicted and sentenced for offences connected with the emergency in Northern Ireland. Twenty-six of them are serving life sentences. The average length of sentence being served by the rest is about eleven years.
>
> The abolition of hanging in December 1969, after a trial period of five years when it was in suspension, has resulted since 1970, in a doubling of numbers of prisoners with a life sentence. They have risen from 646 to a provisional total of 1,210 on December 6. The increase will continue. They are a volatile ingredient in the prison population.[8]

The recipe for discontent in the prisons is made clear: take a large number of prisoners, house them in old, overcrowded Victorian relics, mix in a handful of long-termers who will stir and shake the prison system. It is a well-tried, and, it is argued, well-proven formula or 'recipe for disaster', as the prison officers frequently describe it. It is used to explain away the increasingly vociferous protests by prisoners, which, in the 1970s have taken the form of massive, peaceful sit-downs and rooftop disturbances, and have been most visible in the summer of 1972, with demonstrations at over one hundred prisons, at Gartree in 1972 and 1977, Hull in 1976, and Wormwood Scrubs in 1979.

But the ingredients need closer examination. That there is a crisis of conditions created by the nature and use of the prison system is clear, and it has been explored in detail in chapters 2 and 3. It is also

---

[7] *Sunday Times*, 23 January 1977.
[8] *The Times*, 13 December 1976.

apparent that there has been an increase in the daily number of long-term prisoners in general, and lifers in particular. But, as King and Morgan point out, the increase in long-term prisoners, from 3,678 in 1962 to 5,196 in 1977 (forty-one per cent) has been accompanied by a spectacular increase in the number of maximum security places. They argue that there are now as many as 3,500 maximum security places (5,833 per cent increase), though the Home Office puts the figure at 2,000 (a 3,333 per cent increase from 1962 to 1977).[9]

Moreover, the portrayal of life sentence prisoners as 'prisoners with nothing to lose' is misleading. Life sentence prisoners, other than the relatively few with long minimum recommendations, have everything to lose. They can only be released on licence and are well aware of their dependence upon good reports by the prison authorities to the Parole Board. In contrast, prisoners with fixed sentences can quantify the possible loss of remission in deciding whether to join in prisoners' protests. Thus, for example, in April 1981, a jury in the coroners court at Birmingham decided that Barry Prosser, a prisoner in Winson Green had been unlawfully killed by a blow which was delivered with such force that it burst his stomach and oesophagus. A former prisoner alleged that he had been told by a prison officer that if he kept quiet about the incident he could be released later in the year. The prisoner further testified that after Prosser's death all the prisoners in the hospital area of the jail were moved out to other prisons. The recent upsurge in protests by prisoners can hardly, therefore, be explained away solely in terms of the actions of prisoners with nothing to lose! It is not only lifers who are prepared to demonstrate and make public their criticism of prison regimes.[10]

The claim that the increase in long-term prisoners is related to the abolition of capital punishment, needs to be challenged, for the build-up of long-term prisoners dates not from the abolition of hanging, but can be traced throughout the period 1960-67. The argument that if capital punishment were still in use the crisis of containment would not exist, or at least would be substantially reduced, is also implausible. For this to have happened a large

---

[9]King and Morgan, 1980, 79.
[10]*Guardian*, 16 April 1981.

number of people now serving long sentences would have to have been executed in the past twelve years. The previous use of the death penalty suggests that this would not have occurred. Since 1900, for example, forty-five per cent of all death sentences have been commuted to life imprisonment.[11]

It is not our concern here to enter into a debate about capital punishment, but to argue that the increasing use of long-term imprisonment can be causally related to the abolition of hanging, is clearly untenable. To re-introduce capital punishment, and even to enact it retrospectively, would not have significant impact on the increasing long-term prison population. We must look beyond the abolition of a little-used mode of punishment, and its questionable deterrent effects, to explain this increase. In particular, we need to examine changes in sentencing policy, the impact of parole, the increasing length of time served by lifers, the changing nature and perceptions of crime, and the substantial increases in the number of private and public police, their organization, methods and activities. In other words, the crisis of containment in the prisons has its source neither in the characteristics of the imprisoned population, nor in the abolition of capital punishment. Rather it is a crisis which has developed in particular out of the policies and practices of the prison system, and, more generally, out of wider changes in the nature of law and order and its implementation beyond the prison walls.

But the individuals who structure and manage the daily life of the prisons are generally uninvolved in either the creation of policy within the penal system, or wider debates about law and order. Inevitably, they define and respond to 'problem situations' of daily management only in terms of the immediate context of these situations.

Prisoners' protests, however large or small, are thus seen as the work of a minority of 'troublemakers' who provoke discontent among an otherwise quiescent prison population. Official insistence on this 'one bad apple in an otherwise OK barrel' theory has fuelled the crisis of containment. Recent protests by prisoners have focussed attention on the inadequacies of this theory. The prison authorities have a number of standard responses to such protests. Firstly, they cover them up, trying to deny that they have happened, or, failing

---

[11]*The Times*, 10 December 1976.

this, refuse to disclose information about them. Secondly, the validity of prisoners' complaints are ignored in the rush to identify the 'ring leaders' and to isolate them and their alleged influence. The outcome of such protests, then, is not an inquiry into the complaints of prisoners, but rather a hardening and extension of the apparatus of security and control. In this way, the prison authorities are actively creating and recreating the very conditions which give rise to protest.

PHYSICAL SECURITY

Physical security is the most visible part of the system of control apparatus, and is a major focus of discussion about containing the imprisoned. The 1966 *Report of the Inquiry into Prison Escapes and Security* has been used to justify the concern with security and control. The Mountbatten Report was generally complemented in its emphasis on physical containment by the 1968 Radzinowicz Report on *The Regime for Long-Term Prisoners in Conditions of Maximum Security*, although there were crucial differences which we will examine in chapter 5. However, it should be noted that the policy of security and control which Mountbatten recommended was very much in line with existing prison department policies, and in no way represented an abrupt change in official penal thinking. The department, for example, had already drawn up plans for a maximum security block which was to include 'floodlighting, televisual and electronic aids . . . an uninterrupted, reinforced concrete wall, thirty feet high with an inward and outward overhang, surrounded by dead ground planted with anti-tank blocks and further enclosed by a chain-link fence'.[12] Entry to the block would be by underground tunnel.

King and Elliott have described the growth of physical security at Albany prison on the Isle of Wight. Opened in 1967, Albany had originally been built to house low-security prisoners. The buildings had been so designed as to include physical security, obviating the need for strong perimeter fences. Within four months of its opening, work began on the erection of a seventeen-foot perimeter fence in readiness for the Category B prisoners, which it had subsequently been decided Albany would hold. In January 1969, when this fence

---

[12]King and Elliott, 1977, 24.

was completed, work immediately began on the construction of a second fence, some twenty feet inside the first.[13]

The second fence had been erected by October 1970. Both fences had an overhang ?t the top, and were surmounted by barbed wire. The area between them was surfaced, and geophonic alarms installed:

> which could be triggered when the fences were approached from inside . . . Along the length of the fence, and at various points in the yards, including the sportsfields, floodlights were fixed eighty feet high at the top of masts, the bases of which were concreted into the ground. The lights flooded the yard and perimeter so that television cameras, also mounted on masts, could survey both the inner and outer fences by night as well as during the day . . . Strengthened accommodation was provided for gatehouse staff, who were now protected by bandit-proof glass. A modern PABX telephonic communications system was installed. New vehicle gates were introduced to the vehicle compound and the main gates were to be motorized.[14]

Within the prison, wherever prisoners had access, manganese steel bars replaced the original mild steel ones. The control room, used for both routine and emergency procedures, housed:

> a generator, two-way radio equipment, the television monitors, a master location panel for the prison, and would in time contain a computer and the control panels for the central automatic control system. It was surrounded by a chain link security fence, and staffed by teams of four officers drawn from a group under the leadership of a senior officer. The expanded perimeter defence force, including five fixed observation posts and a prison dogs section now numbering twelve dogs and their handlers, provided routine coverage of the prison. They maintained regular UHF contact with control, using special call signs to indicate the nature of any incidents. Alarm devices

---

[13]ibid., 26-8.
[14]ibid., 170.

were fitted to staff quarters so that off-duty officers could be called back to the prison in cases of emergency. And plans were drawn up whereby the staff from the three island prisons, Camp Hill, Parkhurst and Albany, as well as the local police could be speedily mobilized in the event of an escape or serious disturbance.[15]

These sorts of security improvements were simultaneously being introduced at almost every other closed prison. Such devices as lights and cameras were in evidence before the Mountbatten Report, which facilitated the extension and intensification, but not the genesis of the concern with containment. Wally Probyn, for example, described his pasage into a top-security wing in 1966, entry to which was constantly monitored by cameras:

> We reached the door and the screw unlocked the heavy outer iron gate and then pressed a button at the side of the wall. A metallic voice spoke from the speaker under the button. The screw replied and pulled back the lever of the inner electronically operated door. The outer door clanged shut and was locked. The inner door crashed into place and I found myself entombed in a small space surrounded by bullet-proof observation panels. The screw pressed another button and spoke into the speaker, a face appeared at the electronic control-room observation panel and then disappeared, a voice spoke and the screw pulled back the lever of the inner electronic door. We stepped into a short darkened corridor and then a door slammed shut.[16]

INTERNAL CONTROL

Mountbatten had envisaged that the extension of perimeter security would lead to a more relaxed regime within the walls. In practice, security and control have had as great an impact on daily lives inside the prisons as on the exterior walls.

---

[15]ibid., 171.
[16]Probyn, 1977, 107.

In discussing internal control we want to separate out what we will call *individual* from *collective* forms of control. The two clearly overlap and this separation is used simply as a device for organizing our discussion of a feature of containment. In examining individual control we will focus on the use of punishments, remission and parole, and, in looking at collective control, we will discuss segregation within prisons and the use of particular units and regimes for prisoners identified as 'troublemakers'.

We have already explored the types and methods of punishment and the use of remission in prison. In chapter 3, we showed that there were both formal and informal methods of punishment designed to enforce conformity to the rules and regulations of penal establishments.

We also described the system of remission which operates, again, in the interests of establishing and maintaining internal control. Remission has long been a feature of the prison system, and in 1921, Ruggles-Brise commented on the importance of remission in securing control in the prisons:

> Moreover, the risk of fear of losing remission marks operates as a powerful deterrent against idleness or misconduct and it has been found, generally, that under the influence of this salutary provision, there has been a marked improvement in the tone and demeanour of the prisoners, while, at the same time, an aid has been furnished to those responsible for maintaining order and discipline.[17]

Even earlier, the Governor of Northampton prison noted in his report of 1907-8 that remission:

> tends to strengthen a Governor's hand in maintaining discipline, and gives him an alternative punishment to the 'well-worn' bread and water diet, for which I am thankful.[18]

Since then the importance of this role has increased as sentences have become longer. In 1979, in England and Wales, 16,838 punishments

---

[17]Ruggles-Brise, 1921, 81.
[18]Cited in Thomas, 1972, 133.

of loss of remission were 'awarded' to male prisoners.[19] Loss of remission was the punishment most frequently awarded to male prisoners (stoppage of earnings was most frequently used for women prisoners).

Parole is the most recent addition to the armoury of individual control. Introduced in the Criminal Justice Act of 1967, parole began operating in 1 April 1968. Officially, the basic philosophy of parole is that:

> Long periods in custody, far from fitting offenders for re-entry into society, are likely progressively to unfit them; and that some prisoners who do not of necessity have to be detained for the protection of the public are more likely to be made into decent citizens if. before completing the whole of their sentence, they are released under supervision with the liability to recall if they do not behave.[20]

Prisoners serving a fixed term of imprisonment of over eighteen months are eligible to be considered for parole when they have completed one third of their sentence, or twelve months, whichever expires the latter. The procedure is complicated. Unless they decline to be considered for parole, prisoners are first considered by a Local Review Committee (LRC) at the prison where they are held. The LRC must have at least five members, including the prison governor, a probation officer, a member of the Board of Visitors, and two 'members of the public'. If the LRC recommends parole, the prisoner's case is sent to the Parole Board (except for certain categories of offenders who, under the 1972 Criminal Justice Act, can be released by the Home Secretary on the recommendation of the LRC). The Parole Board is allegedly an independent body which considers suitability for parole, and makes a recommendation to the Home Secretary. There are thirty-six members of the Parole Board, who normally work in a group of five, including a judge, psychiatrist, probation officer and criminologist. Few members of the Board are unconnected with the criminal justice system: most are directly employed by it. It is only the Home Secretary who has the power to

---

[19]*Prison Statistics, England and Wales*, 1979: Table 9.2.
[20]*Prisons and the Prisoner*, 1977: Paragraph 108.

release a prisoner on parole, although 'no prisoner sentenced to a fixed term of imprisonment may be released on parole licence unless the Board recommends.'[21] The licence prescribes the conditions of parole and when a person is adjudged to be in breach of these conditions he or she can be recalled to serve out the remainder of the sentence. The Home Secretary has the right to revoke a parole licence at any time, without explanation. In 1977, 10.3 per cent of people paroled in England and Wales had their licence revoked.[22]

Parole is not a right but a privilege, and the cases of prisoners eligible for parole are reviewed annually. The whole process is unnecessarily cumbersome, bureaucratic and drawn out. From the initial review by the LRC to the decision being revealed to the prisoner, up to six months can elapse. During this time, the prisoners are kept in suspense, believing that any misdemeanour in the interim period might affect the ultimate outcome, and lose their parole.

Throughout the whole proceedings, the only direct contact prisoners have with those considering their case is a short interview with a member of the LRC, and the opportunity to state in writing the reasons why they think they should be paroled. Prisoners are given no reason for being refused parole, nor can they have access to or challenge the various reports made about them which the Parole Board considers. These reports are made out by prison officers, medical officers, prison psychologists, governors, the probation and social work services and the police, and any remarks made by the judge at the time of sentence, and press reports of the court proceedings can also be used. The final decision is relayed to the governor, who is asked to inform the prisoners. There is no appeal against the decision.

While conformity to the prison regime does not automatically guarantee parole, prisoners are officially informed that people who misbehave or 'cause trouble' will not be recommended. In the *Abstract of the Rules and Regulations for Convicted Prisoners (Scotland)*, Rule 37, advises:

No prisoner is entitled to parole, nor will he be automatically released on parole. Parole cannot be earned simply by keeping

---

[21]ibid.
[22]*Report of the Work of the Prison Department in England and Wales*, 1977: Paragraph 69.

out of serious trouble in prison, although prisoners guilty of serious misconduct are unlikely to be paroled.[23]

This was underlined by the Home Secretary in his revised guidelines for parole presented to the Parole Board in 1975:

> If a prisoner shows, commonly by bad prison behaviour, refusal to co-operate with anyone trying to help him . . . then he must be regarded as having forfeited parole by his current conduct and attitude.[24]

Given the nature of the process, the uncertainty it causes, and the uses made of it by the prison authorities to enforce compliance, it is not surprising that parole is the focus for much of the discontent experienced by prisoners.

Parole was originally introduced in the belief that there comes a time when many prisoners, especially those serving long sentences, reach a 'peak in their training', beyond which it is inadvisable to hold them. But there is no evidence to support this belief, and much evidence to the contrary. There are no grounds for believing, for example, that a person sentenced to three years can reach the peak of training after one year, but that a person serving thirty years cannot possibly reach that peak until ten years. As we showed in chapters 2 and 3, there is little evidence of any training in prisons for prisoners to reach a peak in. There is also little doubt that the introduction of parole, like the introduction of remission, has reinforced the trend towards lengthening sentences. In discussing the impact of remission on sentencing, Rupert Cross has suggested that the extension of remission may have been one cause of the significant increases in the average length of sentences between 1938 and 1958: 'Even if remission is something which the judge ought not to take into account . . . it is difficult to believe that an increase in its amount would have no effect on sentencing over a period.'[25] Merlyn Rees,

---

[23]*Abstract of the Rules and Regulations for Convicted Prisoners (Scotland)*: Rule 37.
[24]*Report of the Work of the Parole Board in England and Wales*, 1975: Paragraph 30.
[25]Cross, 1971.

former Home Secretary agrees with Cross.[26] Similarly, while it is clear that the tendency towards very long sentences predates the introduction of parole, the scheme has served to reinforce it, and judges, in passing sentence, frequently refer to the possibility of parole as a justification for imposing long sentences.

Parole has come to dominate the lives of many prisoners, particularly those serving long sentences, for whom it holds out the only possibility of an early release. But the harnessing of the parole system to the concerns and dictates of containment emphasizes how individual forms of control operate within the prisons. For prisoners who conform to the prescribed rules, parole is a possible reward. In contrast, those who do not conform will lose their remission, forfeit their chance of parole, and are likely to find themselves defined as 'troublemakers' and subjected to more collective forms of control.

'Collective' control refers to the segregation of prisoners within the prison. The idea of isolating prisoners either on an individual or group basis has long been a traditional feature of the prison system. Under what was known as the 'separate system', for example, the prison authorities went to great lengths to prevent prisoners communicating with each other. While this segregation was officially linked to ideas about training and treatment, it was in essence a means of discipline and control within penal establishments. *The Fifth Report of the Prison Commissioners*, published in 1847, for example, commented:

> The result of our entire experience is the conclusion that the separation of one prisoner from another is the only basis on which a reformatory discipline can be established with any hope of success . . . We feel warranted in expressing our firm conviction that the moral results of the discipline have been most encouraging and attended with a success which we believe is without parallel in the history of prison discipline.[27]

What concerned the prison authorities the most was their fear of the moral contamination of one prisoner by another, a fear which is still found in contemporary penal practices, most visibly in the

---

[26]*Hansard*, 1 August 1980: Column 1919.
[27]Cited in Playfair, 1971, 61-2.

separation of men from women, and adults from young offenders. But it is also implicit in much of the present concern about 'troublemakers' and their 'subversive' influence on the general prison population, which has led to demands for even more segregation and collective control in penal establishments. For example, Robert Mark, former Metropolitan Police Commissioner, has argued that the dispersal system has produced 'the worst of all possible worlds, with our most hardened criminals enjoying extensive opportunity to contaminate the rest of the prison population'.[28] Prison officers are perhaps the most consistent and vociferous campaigners for increasing segregation. In their evidence to the *Royal Commission on the Penal System in England and Wales* in 1965, for example, they argued for a 'phased' system of imprisonment which would segregate different types of prisoners:

> Strenuous efforts should be made using every means possible to separate the various types of prisoners and to work out different regimes for them. To achieve this end might be that the curriculum of the large local prisons should be phased. In every prison the characteristics of the inmates are about the same, for most of them are purely inadequates. Only a small proportion, probably less than one tenth, of the men in any particular prison are of the vicious, trouble-making type. These are the men who exert a baleful influence over the remainder, if these troublemakers were housed in a special part of the prison (to be known perhaps as the 'maximum security wing') they could then be treated under strict maximum security.[29]

Prison officers have been extremely critical of such maximum security wings, and of successive Home Secretaries' refusals to build a single fortress-type institution for all maximum security prisoners. While there may be dispute how to contain them, there is considerable unanimity among prison staff and prison authorities that 'troublemakers' can be identified as responsible for the present

[28]Cited in Evans, 1980, xi.
[29]Cited in *Royal Commission on the Penal System in England and Wales*, Vol. III, 1965, 97.

unrest in prisons, and should be segregated because of their
influence on the rest of the prison population.

Segregation, then is a central feature of imprisonment, and has
become the predominant method of dealing with 'troublemakers'.
As Cohen has pointed out, although the Government has so far
rejected calls for the concentration of 'troublesome' and maximum-
security prisoners in a single institution, the official policy of
dispersal:

> should not hide the fact that considerable concentration is
> already a feature of the system. This takes place in at least three
> ways: first, through the formal categorization of types of
> prisoners in terms of danger and security-risk, and the
> particular existence of the Category A group who are subject to
> severe and special restrictions and deprivations; second,
> through the setting up of concentrated separate institutions;
> and third, the segregation of offenders *within* the institution:
> in punishment blocks, isolation cells, etc.[30]

Cohen argues that these arrangements are by no means accidental;
rather they represent the essence of the penal system:

> For whatever the ultimate aims of imprisonment – as discussed
> in conferences, newspaper editorials, Parliament, the judiciary
> – the daily task of managers of the system is to maintain
> security through the prevention of escapes and disturbances
> . . . the nightmare of the officials is that there should be
> trouble; to quote one Home Office administrator: 'If I get to
> the end of the day and the telephone hasn't rung, it's been a
> good day.'[31]

It is the *logic* of containment, then, that prisoners who threaten to
or who actually disturb the prison routine should be simultaneously
segregated and concentrated in separate units away from the rest of
the prison population.

It is this logic which dictates that it is the people who do not fit in

---

[30]Cohen, 1977, 221.
[31]ibid.

with and accept the regimes in prison who are the problems, rather than the regimes themselves. In consequence, the policy of containment in the prison system has never been questioned.

Traditionally, physical force has been the major method of punishing prisoners who resist 'good order and discipline'. Flogging and birching were used until 1962 in England and Wales, and corporal punishment was formally abolished only in 1967.[32] Prisoners who offend against prison rules and regulations can be subject to cellular confinement in the punishment block, although, as we showed in chapter 3, provision is also made under Rule 43 in England and Wales, and Rule 36 in Scotland for 'troublesome' prisoners to be held in solitary confinement. Rule 36 in Scotland reads:

> If at any time it appears to the Visiting Committee or the Secretary of State that it is desirable for the maintenance of good order or discipline, or in the interests of a prisoner, that he should not be employed in association with others, the Visiting Committee or the Secretary of State may authorise the Governor to arrange for him to work in a cell, and not in association, for a period not exceeding one month from the date of each authorization.[33]

In practice, prisoners can be held indefinitely in solitary confinement, authorized month by month.

Prisoners 'awarded' cellular confinement are usually taken to the punishment block, which is either housed in the wing, or is a purpose-built building, now known as the 'segregation unit'. Prisoners can be confined on the wing landings if the punishment block is full. Each dispersal prison in England and Wales has a segregation unit. Prisoners on punishment are held in solitary confinement except for slopping out and exercise. Whenever cell doors are opened, a minimum of two 'discipline' prison officers are present. Meals are taken in the cell, which is bare except for a mattress and bedding (removed during the day) and a chamber pot. Work, usually sewing mailbags, can be provided. Writing and reading materials are restricted. For example, prisoners may have

---

[32]Thomas, 1972, 201.
[33]*Prison Rules, Scotland*, 1952: Rule 36.

access to a selection of books in the 'library' of the punishment block. On 'library day' a prisoner brings the available books around on a trolley, but many prisoners on punishment will not borrow books, which are usually badly damaged, and missing pages. Not only is it frustrating to read a book only to find pages have been removed, but prisoners run the risk of being put on report for damaging prison property when the book is handed back, even if pages were missing or the book damaged when they received it.

'Strip' cells are also used on the punishment block. In these, prisoners are left naked in a completely bare cell, and there is often a 'strong box' or 'silent cell' which is a cell within a cell, and is dark, padded and effectively sound-proofed. Prisoners in the punishment block are visited each day by the governor and the medical officer.

It is 'down the Block' that physical violence is most common, and prisoners are most likely to be assaulted by prison staff. It is widely known, if not officially sanctioned, that violence is commonplace in the 'Block'. Prisoners' and ex-prisoners' accounts of what happens in the punishment cells constantly refer to beatings, thumpings and brutality on the part of the prison officers. Jimmy Boyle wrote of life in a Scottish punishment block:

> I lay in solitary for four months awaiting trial and experienced moments of downright despair listening to the screws beating up guys who were being brought into the solitary block. I would have preferred to have been involved in the trouble rather than being in a concrete box hearing the sound of the thuds. At times like this the other prisoners would get up to their doors and bang them constantly, shouting for the dirty bastards to leave the guy alone. This is all one can do as one is in a completely helpless position having to listen to the blows thumping into him, his moans and occasional screams. The whole process is deeply humiliating to everyone. Most prisoners, when they are beaten up, just curl into a ball and accept what is given out as they know that to retaliate will lead to them being charged by the cops which would only lead to an additional sentence.[34]

---

[34]Boyle, 1977, 174.

Boyle continues:

> Most people have preconceived ideas about prisoners so when
> it comes to a direct confrontation of believing the screws
> or the prisoner, then the latter is usually the loser.[35]

In 1977, cellular confinement was 'awarded' to prisoners on
2,707 occasions in England and Wales.[36] While cellular confinement
is the major method of segregation for individual prisoners, units
for 'extra' punishment of 'troublemakers' have recently been
developed. Such units are explicitly designed to break the spirit
of certain prisoners. The most notorious of these were the control
units in England and Wales and the 'cages' in Scotland.

The control units were set up in response to the massive
demonstrations by prisoners in 1972. Two units with special regimes
were planned, at Wakefield and Wormwood Scrubs, although
only the one at Wakefield had been used. According to Circular
Instruction 35/1974, control units were designed to:

> relieve dispersal prisons, for limited periods and as occasion
> arises, from the pressure and strains imposed by the activities
> and influence of the small minority of prisoners who from
> time to time deliberately set out to undermine and disrupt
> the pattern of life of the prison in which they are held,
> and show by their repeated behaviour that they are determined
> not to co-operate with the normal training regime. This
> will be done by removing any such prisoner to the unit
> until such time as he is able to show his willingness to
> behave himself and the ability to sustain that good behaviour
> for a substantial period of time, within the framework
> of the regime of the unit.[37]

Only the 'deliberate and persistent troublemaker' is to be sent
to the unit, where the regime is 'designed both to reduce the
opportunities for continued disruptive behaviour and bring

---

[35]ibid., 175.
[36]*Prison Statistics, England and Wales,* 1977: Tables 9.2 and 9.3.
[37]Circular Instruction Prison Department, Home Office, 35, 1974.

troublemakers to a realization that it is only by mending their ways that return to normal conditions can be achieved.'[38]

A prisoner who has shown himself to 'have the intention of deliberately subverting the regime and the capability of actually disrupting the normal running of the establishment in which he is contained' would be eligible. Control units were designed as the stage beyond segregation units, and, as the Circular Instruction made clear, it would be 'exceptional for a control unit to be considered suitable for a man who has not previously been located in a segregation unit or transferred either within a dispersal system, or for short periods to a local prison'. Prisoners did not actually have to cause trouble to be eligible for the units: 'a prisoner with a past history of successful and severely disruptive troublemaking might be considered for admission as a preventive measure if there were a clear indication that he was intent on repeating this behaviour, even if matters had not reached the point of actual disruption'.[39]

The regime in the units was 'intentionally austere'. Contact between prisoners and staff was reduced to a minimum, to reduce 'the opportunity for confrontation between prisoners'. The regime was divided into two, three-month stages. In stage 1, prison life was reduced to the barest statutory minimum. Prisoners would not be compelled to work, but the Circular Instruction points out that 'until and unless he does, he will not even begin to qualify for the second stage.' Only after three months of continuous good behaviour will the prisoner enter stage 2. The second stage, also lasting three months, provided a 'modest element of activities designed to test the prisoner's willingness and ability to sustain good behaviour in associated conditions, i.e. to resist the temptation to resort to the kind of misbehaviour that got him sent to the control units in the first place.' In stage 2 the prisoner had a 'measure of activity' in association with other prisoners.

It was made clear to the prisoner that there would be regular tests of his willingness to co-operate, 'by performing regular work, both in his cell and in the company of others, and by not causing trouble'. A prisoner who failed to work or attempted to cause trouble would revert back to day 1, stage 1, and serve his time again.

---

[38]ibid.
[39]ibid.

The control units were explicitly punitive: 'there is no expectation that it will cure prisoners wanting to stir up trouble; only demonstrate to them that it does not pay them to do so.' Prisoners who misbehaved on their return to normal prison life, would be sent back to the units.

Control of admission to the units rested with the prison department. The governor of any prison could apply for a particular prisoner to be sent to the unit. This application would be considered first by the regional director, and then passed on to the Control Units Committee set up in the Central Prison Department. Again, it was this committee alone which could authorize the discharge of a prisoner from the units. In reaching their decision, the committee would consider not only the 'objective test of good behaviour for the required period', but also assessments from prison staff of the prisoner's response to the unit. Prison staff were to receive special training in how not to communicate with prisoners, particularly crucial in stage 1.

Public protests about the inhumane conditions in the control units forced the Home Secretary to announce, in March 1975, a temporary suspension of their use. But the Home Secretary's announcement was carefully worded: 'no prisoners are at present being considered for transfer to the unit, but the accommodation will continue to be available for use should the need arise.'[40] Fears of penal reform groups that the control units would be used again were justified when in May 1975 *Working People,* a newspaper concerned with developments in the prison system, published evidence that three more men had been sent to the Wakefield unit.[41]

The campaign against the units was stepped up, and on 24 October 1975, the Home Secretary announced, for the second time, the temporary closure of the units. Again he made it clear that the control units would still be available for use if the need were to arise. He also extended the number of cells available in local prisons for the accommodation of 'troublemakers' for a short 'cooling off' period. Since the demise of the control units the use of segregation and of drugs to control prisoners has been extended. Demands for the reopening of the control units have been frequently made, and the

---

[40]*Hansard,* 3 March 1975: Column 322.
[41]*Working People,* May 1975.

history of the 'cages' in Scotland, reopened in 1978 after six years of non-use provides a salutary lesson in what happens when such units are 'suspended' rather than closed down altogether.

The segregation unit at Porterfield prison, Inverness, known as 'the cages' was introduced in 1966. Like the control units, they were designed for 'troublemakers' who 'contaminated' other prisoners:

> A segregation unit exists at Inverness prison (Porterfield) to accommodate known troublemakers. The type of prisoner likely to qualify is one who has a bad influence on other inmates, persistently refuses to co-operate or exerts generally a subversive influence in the prison to which he has been allocated.[42]

Officially 'the regime in this unit, which has a high degree of security, is strict and privileges are reduced to the minimum.'[43]

Prisoners were originally meant to be held for three months, to be taught a 'short, sharp lesson', but a number of prisoners served very much longer, including Jimmy Boyle who served twenty-two months in one of the five cages in the unit. The physical layout of the cages was described by a journalist who visited them when they were empty:

> Your bed, on the cold bare stone floor, is a solid four-inch-high fixed board in the corner. Only at nights do you get a mattress, pillow and army-type blankets.
>
> In the opposite corner is a fixed white bollard seat in front of a small angled table fixed on to the wall and cage bars.
>
> In the other corner a plastic baby-sized potty with the considerate touch of a plastic lid for overnight use.
>
> And that's it.
>
> That's all the prisoner has in his 'inmate area' as it's called . . . in the Cage the officers on duty yesterday kept referring to it as 'the room'.
>
> Someone locked in the Cage can pace up and down to pass the time.

---

[42]*Prisons and other penal establishments in Scotland,* 1978, 13.
[43]*Prisons in Scotland,* 1966, 6.

Four steps from side wall to side wall, three steps from bars to back wall . . . up and down, back and forward.

The heavy one-inch thick bars stretch from ceiling to floor with a five inch gap at the base. Just enough for the prisoner's food tray to be slid underneath on the floor, if necessary. All meals are eaten in the Cage. The Cage door itself has no keyhole – it is locked and unlocked by a security device outside in the corridor of the unit. The only mirror – armour-plated at that – is on the wall facing the Cage door, in the other half of the room known as the 'cell service area'. Here too is the only window, but you can't see anything through the heavy, double-glazed, opaque window with a security wire grille. Above is a strip light, and alongside it a small roof light that's on day and night. The door to the cell has the normal peep-hole, but also a special angled fish-eye spy hole that looks across into the Cage itself.[44]

Jimmy Boyle has provided an account of what it was like to be held in them:

The caged area is approximately 9 ft. by 6 ft. The only moveable objects besides the human body are a small plastic chamberpot – lidless, a woollen blanket and one book that is issued each week. Human contact is made three times a day when the 'screws' enter to search the body of the prisoner. His mouth, armpits, anus and the soles of his feet are searched each time even though he could not have left the cell between searches. This humiliation and degradation takes place daily. There is no communication between the 'screws' and the prisoners. He is alone and at the complete mercy of the 'screws' who take full advantage of his helplessness. Brutality and abuse of human rights is rife. If a prisoner is particularly awkward then punishment takes the form of leaving his food just out of reach behind the cage bars until it is cold, or he receives it with spittle in it.[45]

---

[44]*Daily Record,* 15 November 1978.
[45]Cited in MacDonald and Sim, 1978, 23-4.

Use of the cages was suspended after December 1972, when there was a riot in the segregation unit, during which several prison officers and prisoners were severely injured. Four prisoners later received sentences of up to six years for assaulting prison staff. No officers were charged. At the end of 1978, the cages were once more in use, after a vociferous public campaign for their re-opening by prison officers, including a work-to-rule which threatened to bring chaos to the Scottish prison system. We will examine this campaign and motives behind it in the next chapter.

The central irony of units such as punishment blocks, control units and cages is that normal prison life, itself the source of much discontent and of 'troublemakers', becomes the goal to be sought after, a reward for good behaviour. The validity of prisoners' protests against the prison regime is ignored in the rush to identify 'troublemakers' and to segregate them from the rest of the prison population.

When the prison regime itself is questioned the logic of control is sometimes challenged. This happened in the early 1970s, and led to the opening of the Special Unit at Barlinnie prison. The Special Unit was established following the report of a Working Party, set up by the Scottish Home and Health Department, to inquire into the *Treatment of Certain Male Long Term Prisoners and Potentially Violent Prisoners*. Unlike any such report before, or since, and in marked contrast to Circular Instruction 35/1974 which set up the control units in England and Wales, the Working Party openly acknowledged the role of the exisiting systems of dealing with long term prisoners in creating 'troublemakers'. As the Report, dated 1971, argued, 'the basic reason for violence in prisons is imprisonment.'[46] Moreover, the Working Party, despite its title, stressed its concern to avoid using labels such as 'troublemaker', 'subversive', 'psychopath', which spring all too easily to the lips of prison staff, prison department officials, MPs and others who comment on prisoners' protests. Reporting in 1971, the Working Party recognized that regimes such as the cages were directly responsible for increasing the violence between prisoners and staff. The opening of the Special Unit in February 1973 was not simply a

---

[46]*Report of Treatment of Certain Male Long-Term Prisoners and Potentially Violent Prisoners,* 1971: Paragraph 7.

response to the riot at the cages in December 1972: the riot had underlined the main findings of the Report, and was probably instrumental in the early opening of the Unit at Barlinnie, rather than at Perth as originally recommended.

But as it was originally set up, the Special Unit reflected some of the more unpalatable features of other segregation units, in particular in its traditional psychiatric orientation. It was seen very much as a last chance. If prisoners did not respond to the regime at the Special Unit, the next step for them was to Carstairs, the state mental hospital, without any possibility of a release date. But the original psychiatric basis of the Unit has since been rejected by both prisoners and staff:

Due mainly to the efforts of its staff and prisoners the Special Unit has evolved over its five years into a self-styled therapeutic community. In terms of physical conditions and personal relationships between prisoners and staff the Unit has progressed away from the traditional authoritarian non-relationships and spartan conditions that the majority of long-term prisoners in Scotland face. There is a great deal of freedom, responsibility and personal choice given to prisoners within the confines of the Unit.

The men wear their own clothes rather than prison uniform. They can decorate their own cells and keep books and record players. They can cook their own food, supplementing prison rations with food bought with their own money. Their mail, unlike that of prisoners in the traditional system, is unrestricted and uncensored. Access to visitors is also unrestricted except when the men are locked up at night.

Each prisoner plans his own routine for the day and democratic community meetings take place weekly to discuss any issues that may have arisen. Any member of the community – either staff or prisoner – who 'lets the side down' by breaking the rules, can end up in the 'hot-seat' where his actions are discussed, criticized and chastised by the other members of the community, again whether staff or prisoner.

These weekly meetings function as a place where people learn to talk out any problems they might have in an open and objective way – something which is impossible in the traditional system. When a decision affecting domestic issues has to be made, each man, staff or prisoner, has one vote. One of the earliest and most symbolic taken was to remove the door of the punishment cell, which meant that reliance on the old method of punishing an individual by locking him up in solitary confinement was abandoned in favour of the new community based 'hot-seat'. This, according to both the staff and the inmates, is a much more effective means of control than the measures used in the traditional system, measures which, in the majority of cases, serve only to make the prisoner more resentful and bitter.

Ultimately, it is this ability to make democratic decisions and the positive staff–prisoner relationships, together with a physical environment far removed from the obsolete conditions of the majority of prison buildings, which makes the Special Unit unique.[47]

MEDICINE AND CONTROL

The continued existence and qualified success of the Special Unit at Barlinnie stands in marked contrast to the general direction in which regimes for long-term prisoners are developing.

In particular, the increasing involvement and influence of psychiatric and medical services in the containment of long term prisoners should be viewed with considerable alarm. For what this represents is not simply the use of medical techniques such as drugs to control prisoners, but also the reinforcement of the logic of containment, the unquestioning acceptance of existing penal regimes, and the search for 'troublemakers' and 'subversives'. Psychiatry and medicine, as used in the contemporary prison system, translate structural problems into individual behavioural and medical ones. This trend is most visible in the increasing use of drugs to control prisoners.

That drugs are prescribed in prisons is not in dispute. Dr James Orr, Director of the Prison Medical Service told the *Sunday Times* that Largactil and other major tranquillizers have been used in

---

[47]MacDonald and Sim, 1978, 26-7.

prisons since 1958.[48] The 1973 *Report of the Work of the Prison Department* noted that 'there has been an even greater tendency towards the use of psychotropic drugs in the treatment of psychiatrically disturbed patients.'[49] The amount spent on drugs has increased from £131,327 in 1971-2 to £379,000 in 1977-8. The Home Office has argued that this increase does not suggest over-prescribing but rather reflects 'inflation and rising numbers of prisoners with mental disorders'.[50] Such an explanation stands in marked contrast to the Prison Department's account of a proportionately similar increase in the cost of education in prisons. In this case, the explanation is not rising numbers or inflation, but improved and increased facilities.

The Home Office has claimed consistently that drugs are only administered to prisoners for medical reasons. In reply to questions in the House of Commons, Dr Shirley Summerskill, a junior minister at the Home Office, insisted that prison doctors 'have not and would not practice the use of drugs as an aid to discipline or to control behaviour.' She continued:

> I am also convinced that none of the doctors who work in the Prison Medical Service would respond to requests from prison staff to prescribe drugs for this purpose.[51]

Her comments are surprising given the results of a study of the *Treatment of Psychopaths with Depixol* produced by a former prison doctor, Dr C. H. McCleery, and published in the *Prison Medical Journal*. According to Dr McCleery:

> For some years we have had the problem of containment of psychopaths who, as a result of situational stress, have presented the discipline staff with control problems for which there has been no satisfactory solution . . . From a medical angle those men show no evidence of formal illness as such, but, clearly, are characters having a lot of nervous tension, a certain amount of depression, considerable frustration with a

---

[48]*Sunday Times*, 22 October 1978.
[49]*Report of the Work of the Prison Department in England and Wales*, 1973: Paragraph 212.
[50]*Guardian*, 16 December 1978.
[51]ibid.

low flash point who, until the situational stress can be removed
or modified, are potentially either very dangerous or in the case
of the more inadequate, an unmitigated nuisance.

Dr McCleery added that those men 'are considered by the governor
and discipline staff as medical problems . . . [and were] regarded
purely as discipline failures.'[52]

In this way, prisoners identified as 'troublemakers' (whose
behaviour is not changed by segregation) become 'medical' problems
in need of treatment. Dr Summerskill's denials of the use of drugs to
control prisoners have also been contradicted by a consultant
psychiatrist 'with long experience of prison conditions' interviewed
by the *The Times* in 1977. He remarked that for a Category A
prisoner who needed treatment in an outside hospital 'it might be
reasonable to use tranquillizers to sedate him' to reduce the risk of an
escape.[53] Moreover, as long ago as 1970, the General Secretary of the
Prison Officers' Association pointed out that the use of sedative
drugs was permitted to pacify 'troublemakers' in prisons.[54]

The Home Office also insists that, except in exceptional
circumstances, all drugs are administered to prisoners on a voluntary
basis. The notion of voluntarism is always a difficult one, and in the
penal setting, is extremely suspect. Dr McCleery, for example,
admitted that men only agreed to be injected with Depixol 'after a
lot of persuasion'.[55]

In defending the use of drugs, the Home Office are quick to point
out that many prisoners queue for their daily doses. It is undoubtedly
true that many prisoners prefer to be 'floating on a sea of
tranquillizers' (to quote a part-time medical officer) rather than
having to face the grim reality of daily prison life.[56] But the concept
of voluntarism in the prison system is very dubious; given the fact
and nature of their incarceration, how voluntary is the prisoner's
decision to join the drug queue?

In its 1979 annual report, the Prison Department (England and
Wales) responded to the controversy surrounding the use of drugs in

[52]*Prison Medical Journal,* Winter 1978.
[53]*The Times,* 9 May 1977.
[54]ibid., 5 August 1970.
[55]*Sunday Times,* 22 October 1978.
[56]*The Times,* 23 August 1978.

prison by publishing a table listing the total number of drugs dispensed in thirty prisons during 1979. Tim Owen of Radical Alternatives to Prison has produced a detailed critique of the table, and the information produced in it. Owen argues that the table is misleading in three crucial ways. Firstly, the distinction made between 'Psychotropic', 'Hypnotic' and 'Other Drugs Affecting the Central Nervous system' is unclear in that there is no indication of which things are classified in which category. The same drug, depending on usage, may appear in more than one category. Some barbiturates, for example, taken during the day to sedate a prisoner would be classified as psychotropic drugs, but used at night to induce sleep would be classified as 'hypnotic'. Secondly, the broad categorization used by the Home Office disguises the differences between drugs. Thus it is impossible to distinguish between a relatively mild sedative, like Nitrozepan (Mogadon), and an addictive, more dangerous drug such as Amylobarbitone (Amytal). Thirdly, by placing prisons together in groups from two to forty-two, it is impossible to make accurate and meaningful comparisons of doseage rates.'[57]

The publication of the table is an indication of the pressure exerted on the Department. While it is to be welcomed cautiously we need much fuller information before we can discuss the nature and extent of drug use in British prisons. For the moment, we can only agree with Christopher Price, MP, who has concluded:

> I am quite satisfied that there are cases in prisons where doctors are prescribing drugs not for the prisoner's well-being, but for that of the prison regime.[58]

Our concern, though, is not only with such uses and abuses of drugs. After all – and this makes the Home Office's insistent denials more puzzling – it is well known that drugs such as those administered in prisons are widely available and used outside the prison walls. In 1978, for example, some £10 billion was spent in Britain on tranquillizers, and the drug companies emphasize the capabilities of their drugs to control behaviour in much of their

---

[57]RAP Briefing Paper, 1980.
[58]*Guardian*, 5 December 1977.

advertising.[59] What concerns us more is the medicalization of control in prisons: the definition of 'troublesome' behaviour as a medical problem in need of a medical solution, for this represents a new and potentially sinister development in the logic of containment. It is yet another step in the direction of the individualizing and neutralizing of non-conformist behaviour in prisons, and makes the likelihood of a fundamental questioning of the logic of control and its impact on prison life ever more remote.

---

[59] *The Times*, 12 October 1978.

5 KEEPERS OF THE KEYS

> God knows the average prison officer is no paragon of virtue or
> of intellect.[1]

Since 1972, there has been a rapid escalation of protest by prison
officers aimed at improving their pay, conditions and status. The
extent and escalation of disruptive actions taken by prison officers up
to 1978 is fully documented in the Prison Department's evidence to
May. In each year between 1973 and 1975, prison officers took action
on an average of seven occasions. In 1976, the number rose to
thirty-four, in 1977 to forty-two and in 1978 to 114. The number of
institutions involved in these disputes showed a similar increase.
Over fifty different forms of action were taken by officers during this
period, classified by the Home Office into three major groups.
Firstly, actions which interfered with the administration of justice;
for example, refusal to escort prisoners to and from courts, refusal to
allow lawyers, probation officers or police to visit prisoners, and
refusal to act as dock officers in Crown Courts. Secondly, thirty-nine
types of action which interfered with the administration of the
prisons, ranging from the refusal to co-operate with civilian workers,
welfare staff, and disciplinary proceedings and the refusal to allow
workshops to function, to the refusal to fly the flag at half-mast on
the death of Archbishop Makarios. Thirdly, action which directly
interfered with the prison regime, including bans on visits, education
classes, letters, bathing, laundry, and association.[2]

---

[1]Cronin, 1967, 45. Harley Cronin is a former General Secretary of the POA.
[2]*Home Office Evidence to May*, 1979, Vol. 12, 124-5.

As the Home Office points out, there was no coherent pattern to this action but rather it was 'sporadic and unpredictable . . . taken by individual branches often at very short notice and often not lasting long'.[3] As we showed in chapter 1, the most serious action has taken place since the publication of the May Report, and is rapidly becoming an established feature of the contemporary prison system.

Among a group of people with such a strong militaristic and hierarchical tradition, it is perhaps surprising that such a campaign should have been initiated. This reflects the growing concern of many officers that not only are their pay and working conditions poor, but that their job itself is under attack. The monthly letters column of the *Prison Officers' Magazine,* for example, provides ample illustration of their disenchantment with the prison service; disenchantment fuelled by the vociferous protests of prisoners, and by what many prison officers perceive as the insensitivity of the prison authorities to their own complaints. For prison officers, the present crisis in the prisons is not simply about pay and conditions, but is a crisis of authority, revealed in their conflicting relationships with prisoners, other prison staff, Headquarters and even the executive of their own Association. While officers demand to be considered as a 'special case' in their pay negotiations, their militancy reflects more than a concern about money. It raises fundamental questions about the prison system and the role of prison officers within it.

In January 1980 there were 15,882 prison officers in post in England and Wales (including young offender institutions).[4] In Scotland, 1,402 officers were employed on 31 December 1979 in adult penal institutions.[5] There are four prison officer grades; basic, senior, principal and chief. There is usually one chief officer in each establishment who has overall responsibility for the work of prison officers. Each wing is run by a principal officer, with senior officers as their deputies in control of specialist groups of basic grade officers. Such specialisms include security officers, who man the control rooms and gate-houses, and patrol the perimeter walls and fences; hospital officers, responsible for the maintenance of good order and discipline

---

[3]ibid., 119.
[4]*Report of the Work of the Prison Department in England and Wales,* 1979: Paragraph 15.
[5]*Prisons in Scotland,* 1979: Appendix 20.

in the hospital wings, and for assisting the prison medical officer; and trade officers who carry out works services, instructing and supervising prisoners employed in the works department. There are also catering officers, instructors, training officers, physical education instructors, in Scotland clerical officers and, in England and Wales, dog-handlers.

For the majority of basic grade officers, however, work is more generic. One day an officer could be working on the landing of a wing or hall, the next in a workshop as a discipline officer, and the next escorting prisoners to and from court or to another prison. Overall, more than two-thirds of the staff in British prisons are prison officers, most of whom engage in routine, custodial work. The emphasis on security and control has 'added considerably' to this custodial function.[6] Essentially, then, the role of the prison officer is similar to that of the nineteenth century 'turnkey'. As the Prison Officers' Association observed in 1963:

> A day's duty of an officer usually comprises nothing more or less than unlocking the men and locking them up again, escorting them to exercise, to the workshops and back again inside the prison; feeding them and, at the end of the day, finally locking them up and checking them for the night. Indeed, there is little in this procedure that is different from the work of the turnkey in the last century.[7]

Basic grade officers work in shifts. In Scotland, for example, officers are divided into two divisions. The first division will start at 6 a.m. and work until 2 p.m., and the second starts at 2 p.m. and works until 10 p.m. The small night shift is made up of officers from the two divisions. All shifts alternate on a weekly basis, overlapping to ensure that officers are always on duty throughout the day and night. An officer on the first shift, for example, will arrive at the prison around 5.30 a.m. to be ready to take up his post at 6 a.m., just as the night shift workers are coming off. Shifts overlap so that at no time is the prison left unsupervised.

Officers assigned to landing duty on the first shift will start their

---

[6] *Prisons and the Prisoner,* 1977, Paragraph 2.30.
[7] *Prison Officers' Magazine,* November 1963, 330.

day by counting the prisoners in their cells and shouting the numbers on each landing down to the principal officer who checks that all prisoners are accounted for. Cells are unlocked, and officers supervise prisoners' slopping out and breakfast. Prison officers then line up and count prisoners going to work and escort them to the workshops. While prisoners are out of the wing, landing officers will have their own breakfast, supervise the cleaning of the halls, unlock prisoners on report and escort them to the orderly room, and handle new prisoners coming onto the wing. Their next major period of activity is lunchtime, when prisoners return from work to lunch. Again, the emphasis is on counting and standing by, watching prisoners' activities, including exercise. Prisoners are then locked up, and the shifts change. For many officers, then, work is boring, routine and repetitive. This general pattern, with detailed differences, for example in timing, is typical of most prisons in Britain.

It is not surprising, given the daily tasks of prison officers, that recruitment to the basic grades has always proved difficult. In England and Wales, in 1977, for example, the net increase of 299 trained officers fell well short of the planned growth of 850, despite an intensive recruitment drive. In that year, £220,834 was spent on advertising for prison officers, and four selection boards sat full time. While the response to the advertisements was 'very good', with 47,031 enquiries and 13,167 applications being received, the number of successful applicants was, according to the Prison Department, 'disappointingly low', with only 981 men and 163 women joining for training.[8] In 1979, in England and Wales, 703 trained officers were recruited, but 629 left the service.[9]

A person applying for a job as a basic grade officer 'is required to pass an educational test, set by the Civil Service Commission, in English, arithmetic, and general intelligence, a rigorous medical examination, and finally an interview by a Board whose members are experienced prison staff.'[10]

Examples of the types of examination questions are included in

---

[8]*Report of the Work of the Prison Department in England and Wales,* 1977: Paragraph 11.

[9]*Hansard,* 1-7 February 1980: Column 105.

[10]*Prisons in Scotland,* 1977: Paragraph 135.

the official information sheet sent out with application forms. The include:[11]

In Test A (10 minutes), sentences are given with a choice of words in two places. You have to underline the correct words. Example:

    flied   than
1 He flewed to America as this was more convenient from
    flew   in
  going by sea.

    garbage   littring
2 The garbidge was literring the street.
    garrbage   littering

Test B (10 minutes) is designed to show everyday knowledge and practical commonsense. You are given a choice of four different ways to complete an unfinished sentence. Example:

The Morse code was devised to:
1 transmit messages quickly
2 control moral standards in films
3 widen the range of the radio
4 break through the short-wave barrier

Test C (10 minutes) is a general intelligence test. Series of words, letters or numbers are given, and in each question a part is left out, indicated by asterisks (one asterisk for each missing letter of figure). You are meant to discover what is missing. Example:

1 3 6 9 12 15 ** 21
2 Rough smooth   fast slow   rich poor   young ***
3 A BB CCC **** EEEEE

---

[11]The example is cited in Fitzgerald, 1977, 111-12.

Applicants must be British subjects, between 22 and 44½ years old (49½ for women), at least 5 feet 6 inches tall, without shoes (5 feet 3 inches for women). Despite the difficulty in recruiting people to join the Prison Service the POA have resisted any relaxation of these basic entry requirements.

The General Secretary of the POA, has outlined the Association's attempts to raise, rather than lower standards:

> Minimum educational standards for candidates to the Prison Service should be raised to include three O Levels in GCE . . . we feel that the entrance standards are still far too low. The physical standards, which are also important, have actually been reduced in recent years. Before the war, a man had to be 5 ft 8 ins before he was eligible, now he only has to be 5 ft 6 ins. While it is all very well to say that such things should not matter, and that a PO [Prison Officer] should be able to control a prisoner by the strength of his personality, personalities of this sort are not by and large to be found amongst the ranks of the PO. It remains a fact that the 5 ft 6 ins PO looking up at a 6 ft prisoner is in a position of psychological as well as physical disadvantage; whereas if you have a 5 ft 8 ins PO looking down at someone who is 3 ins shorter, the position is reversed.[12]

Initial training for prison officers was revised by a circular instruction in 1978 which argued:

> A more systematic approach is required to basic training, in order to ensure the necessary early opportunities for increasing understanding of human behaviour, man management skills, and technical skills to match demands placed upon staff in the modern prison service.

There are three phases of basic training. Phase 1 is a period of four weeks introduction and 'acclimatization' to the workings of the prison service, when the newly appointed officer is based in one penal establishment. It will include 'some formal instruction and practical experience to a set syllabus. Additionally, although the students will be based at their various joining establishments, the

---

[12] *Cambridge Opinion*, Number 38, 33.

aim of seeking to provide experience in common will be assisted by short attachments to other establishments to ensure that each student gains some awareness of a local prison, a training prison, and a borstal.' Eight weeks is then spent at either of the officer training schools at Wakefield and Leyhill, where 'the course is a generic one with all students receiving the same training irrespective of, and without streaming for, the type of establishment to which they are subsequently posted.' The emphasis is on the organization and practice of the prison service, and includes lectures on self-defence and theories of criminal behaviour. Phase 3, which lasts a week and is spent at the prison where the officer will serve, aims at facilitating 'his introduction to the regime and requirements of that establishment and enabling him to see how the skills he is developing will be used.'[13]

Most officers are heavily critical of this training, which is seen has having little direct relevance to the job on the landing. While training might provide the new recruit with some insight into the workings of the prison system as a whole, it is the experience of working in individual prisons which is more important, since each prison has its own regime, and its officers a particular style of working. This style is very much dependent on the senior, principal and chief officers, all established, long-serving members of the Service. It is their influence rather than the formal training which has the more lasting impact on the new recruit.

Training for specialist roles, such as Training Officer, Security Officer and Control Room staff, is provided at the Prison Service College, as are short courses on staff supervision and prison management, for officers promoted to senior, principal or chief grades.

Pay and conditions of service have been a source of constant complaint among officers, who have taken to disrupting the running of the prisons in pursuit of their demands for improvements. The May Inquiry focused much of its attention on the pay and conditions of uniformed staff. The pay structure of prison officers is extraordinarily complex, including a myriad of allowances and benefits for special duties. As May observed, 'the multiplicity of allowances and the extent to which they are taxable or pensionable

---

[13] *Prison Officers' Magazine,* September 1978, 316-17.

must mean that in a number of cases officers cannot fully understand of what their pay is composed.' Many of the local disputes arose out of the problem of defining exactly who was entitled to what. Shortly after the Inquiry was set up, it was generally agreed that it should act as an arbiter in the long-running dispute over Continuous Duty Credits (CDCs), which are claims in respect of meal breaks taken within duty hours. One of the eleven chapters in the final report was devoted to a detailed exposition of the CDC claims.

But the May Report was more concerned with the general level of pay for prison staff, and in particular their demands for parity with the police, who had just been awarded considerable increases by the 1978 Edmund-Davies Report. It noted that prison officers are among the most isolated groups of public sector workers, and linked this to what it believed to be the unrealistic pay demands of uniformed staff. May argued that 'we have found members of the Service (including governors) to be a somewhat inward-looking group.' This has a number of consequences. Prison officers are 'prone to concentrate on their own terms and conditions of service without a well-informed knowledge of what obtains elsewhere. Further their benefits of what applies outside the prison services tend to be unrealistic as well as restricted.'

In examining the pay claims of the POA the Inquiry was particularly concerned to take account of the special features of the overall payments to staff, including housing allowances, free uniform, non-contributory superannuation benefits, and overtime. The Committee stressed the relatively large amount of overtime worked by officers, underlining that 'it was more than three times as much as that worked by all employees, and over twice that worked on average by manual workers.' Over a million hours a year in overtime was being worked by staff at local prisons and remand centres in England and Wales on court and escort duties alone. The Report had no doubt that the high levels of overtime had a most deleterious effect, not only on individual officers and their families but also on staff/management relationships generally. Through extensive use of overtime, management had become accustomed to stretching manpower to meet extra needs, and staff had become reliant on a higher standard of living.[14]

---

[14]May Report: Paragraph 8.3-8.29.

In order to maintain this standard the Report concludes that some officers known as 'overtime bandits' have attempted 'to manipulate affairs' to obtain high levels of overtime. Moreover:

> Sometimes it almost appears as if there were some sort of collusion between local management and staff, at least to the extent that each group did not in the past look too closely into the motives of the other for co-operating with high overtime demands. It is possible, too, that the high rate of overtime in the last three or four years has been the way in which one part of the public service was informally able to circumvent restrictions on income which would otherwise have followed from incomes policy.[15]

In looking at the evidence as a whole and bearing in mind all the necessary qualifications, the Inquiry concluded that prison officers' pay was at an appropriate level and had not lost any real ground in comparison with other manual workers. In particular, like the Stanhope Report (1923), May explicitly rejected the POA's claim for parity with the police, and concluded that a large pay settlement was not justified.

Average starting salary for a basic grade officer in November 1980 was £143.90 a week, made up of £79.80 basic, a shift allowance of £10.05, a weekend premium of £9.55 and £44.50 overtime. Additionally, there was a separate system of weekly allowances for specialist roles, such as trade instructor, hospital officer, or dog handler. Rent and clothing allowances were also received by officers.[16] All officers worked long hours of financially lucrative overtime. Prison officers have an ambiguous attitude towards overtime, for they complain of the long hours but resist attempts to curtail these. In April 1978, following industrial action protesting at such cutbacks, the Government provided an additional £2 million for the prison department to pay for extra overtime.[17]

Opportunities for promotion to senior grades are limited. Basic grade officers can sit a senior officer's examination, and if they pass,

---

[15]ibid.: Paragraph 6.24.
[16]*Hansard*, 7-13 November 1980: Column 524.
[17]*The Times*, 12 April 1978.

go before a Promotions Board. Successful applicants for senior positions are generally long-serving basic grade officers. The lack of promotion opportunities is a source of discontent among prison officers. Mountbatten, in an effort to increase their promotion opportunities created the post of senior officer, ranking between the basic grades and the principals. But his attempt has served to heighten, rather than diminish prison officers' dissatisfaction with their career structure, as a correspondent to the *Prison Officers' Magazine,* at the end of 1978 made clear:

> Join the modern Prison Service, good prospects for promotion – so the national advertisements state.
>
> I wonder if Lord Mountbatten, when he recommended an intermediate rank between officer and principal officer, i.e. senior officer, could foresee the frustration, disappointment and bitterness it would eventually cause – I doubt it . . . The pressures upon an officer working in a busy local prison are tremendous. Many give years of loyal service working in a building that belongs to the Victorian era. In their precious off-duty time, some of these officers decide to study and prepare themselves for the promotion examination. On having successfully surmounted the first hurdle they await the promotion board. They attend the board and await their fate – *all too often* they are disappointed.
>
> . . . Morale in the Prison Service is dependent on many factors but unless the dedicated officer can expect some recognition for his efforts, the efficiency of the Prison Service will become irrevocably impaired . . . and justifiably so.[18]

THE ROLE OF THE PRISON OFFICER

As the daily routine of prison officers indicates, their major function is containment. The introduction of specialisms has served to reinforce rather than broaden this basic custodial role. Control, then, 'is the common thread which makes it possible to speak generally of the role of the prison officer.'[19] This can be seen not

---

[18]*Prison Officers' Magazine,* November 1978.
[19]*The Criminologist,* November 1970, 110.

only in the nature, but also in the organization of their work.

By tradition, prison officers have been organized on a paramilitary basis, which remains generally intact in the contemporary prison system. Prison officers are organized in a strictly military hierarchical system. At every level of this hierarchy, there are formal limits and delimitations of authority. Each officer has a particular place in the chain of command, and gives and receives orders according to his or her status.

Most officers wear a regulation uniform, with senior ranks distinguished by epaulets and braid on the rim of their hats. Basic-grade officers address seniors as 'Sir', and due deference is publicly demonstrated. Military-style parades used to be commonplace but have declined in recent years. In certain establishments, for example, open prisons, uniforms are no longer worn, but the majority of officers will dress and conduct themselves with a pronounced 'Service' style.

Prison officers' tasks are clearly defined, and discretion, in principle at least, reduced to the minimum. Prison Rules, Standing Orders and Circular Instructions are designed to prescribe a way of handling every possible situation. The system of authority dictates what information is available to each officer, and basic grades are often ignorant of the rules and regulations they are supposed to enforce and to abide by. Orders handed down from above are supposed to be taken unquestioningly:

> In a job of relatively little technical skill, and almost devoid of any theoretical base, one of the substitutes for a body of knowledge is the hoarding of information, often of a very simple kind. Generally, for example, junior prison staff have never been able to have unlimited access to Standing Orders . . . If they have a problem they have to ask a more senior member of the staff for the answer, which is often given unwillingly. Unwillingness to impart information is the most memorable feature of the reception given to newly joined staff.[20]

Paramilitarism is reinforced by the military backgrounds of many

---

[20]Thomas, 1972, 44.

officers. In a sample of 137 prison officers at Strangeways prison, Manchester, in 1970, nearly eighty per cent of officers had had military training of some sort. Most importantly, over ninety per cent of officers who had served five years or more, and thus including those in senior grades, were ex-military, and in a position to impose a particular tradition, set of beliefs and way of working on the slowly increasing number of new recruits who had no military experience.[21] Similarly, in their study of Albany prison, King and Elliott found that ninety-five per cent of senior, and sixty-five per cent of basic grade officers had some type of military training.[22] While there is a decline in the overall number of basic grade officers with military training (due at least in part to the abolition of National Service), the influence of the military remains large in the Prison Service, and new recruits, in their new uniforms, are left in little doubt that it is a *service* which they are joining.

Such paramilitarism is well suited to the basic role of prison officers, but has proved a distinct obstacle to any extension of that role. In particular, it has been an important factor in the marked failure of prison officers to gain responsibility for 'treatment and training' and welfare work in prisons, despite the long, hard campaign for an extension of officers' role by the Prison Officers' Association. The POA, ignoring the history, organization and function of its members, has insisted that prison officers are the people most suited to carry out welfare in the prisons. The General Secretary of the POA, for example, has argued that:

> The facts are that for years the PO (prison officer) has been . . . combining the custodial and supportive aspects of his job and very successfully too. The social worker as such, for example the Welfare Officer, psychiatrist, prison visitor, all of them meet with the same problem, in greater or lesser degree. The prisoner has difficulty in fully accepting them: his typical attitude to them is 'I wonder what they're after?' It is a fact that many of these outside people find it difficult to get down to the level of the ordinary prisoner and really talk to him. Time and again after an interview the prisoner will go to an officer and ask him

---

[21]Colvin, 1978.
[22]King and Elliott, 1977, 203.

the same question – 'what is it all about?' And if he has got a problem then nine times out of ten he will take it to the officer in charge of his particular landing before he will ever think of going to one of those other people. Quite often the officer will refer the problem to those more directly concerned with welfare problems and so break the ice in situations where the prisoner is reluctant to make a direct approach himself. So the fact that the prisoner often turns initially to the PO rather than the welfare staff or voluntary workers shows that there must be a good relationship there.[23]

This line has been repeated for at least fifteen years, and was central to the definitive statement on the 'Role of the Modern Prison Officer', published in the *Prison Officers' Magazine* in 1963:

The work of rehabilitation requires a patient and understanding approach by whoever is engaged in it and an essential part of the work is that the prisoner should feel that someone is interested in him. Those engaged in rehabilitation should be people who are always there and who thoroughly understand the prisoner; people who understand his background outside and his behaviour inside; people who can talk the same language. In the prison world the person who is best fitted to do all these things is the prison officer. It is he and only he who sees the prisoner every minute of his day, who sees him at work and at his recreation. It is the prison officer who because of this personal and constant contact knows the man better than the governor, better than the welfare officer, and it would thus appear logical that he is the man who is mainly concerned with rehabilitation work.[24]

A decade later, the POA called for a 'redoubling of effort by the Department to involve officers to a greater extent in welfare work'.[25] During these ten years, welfare work was assigned to probation officers and social workers, a move which angered the POA, and has been resisted at many levels by prison officers. That prison officers have been engaged in writing more reports on prisoners, for parole,

---

[23] *Cambridge Opinion*, Number 38, 31.
[24] *Prison Officers' Magazine*, November 1963, 332.
[25] ibid., July 1973, 219.

classification and other purposes, is presented as evidence of the willingness and ability of officers to undertake the welfare role. Taking the view that treatment and training are compatible with containment, officers have demanded an extension of casework done by probation officers and social workers to include case conferences at which prison officers would be present and play an active role.

But officers' involvement in welfare, with isolated exceptions, remains minimal in the adult prison system, and the image of the prison officer presented by the POA is idealized. While it might be true that uniformed staff are in a position to have direct daily contact with prisoners, the nature of that contact is hardly conducive to treatment and training.

The ritual unlocking and locking up of prisoners is not conducive to a welfare role, and overcrowding in local prisons makes informal contact even more difficult, assuming it is desired. But ultimately it is the *role* of uniformed staff which militates against their involvement in welfare. Basic-grade officers are duty bound to pass all information about prisoners on to higher authorities, and there can be little confidentiality and trust between prisoner and officer. Prisoners are all too aware that landing officers' verbal and written reports on them can directly influence not only their day-to-day life, but, with parole, even their release date. Orders are shouted to prisoners and reluctance to carry them out with due deference is a punishable offence. Formal power is firmly located in the officers' hands, and, despite the rules and regulations, can be and is used arbitrarily and unpredictably – hardly a situation in which to develop supportive relationships.

Relationships with long-term prisoners are even more fraught. In the most recently built prisons, with electronic systems for unlocking cell doors, face-to-face contact on the landings in the morning is reduced to a minimum. In the electronic coffin of Albany, for example, King and Elliott found that face-to-face contact in A-hall was avoided altogether, 'a fact for which both prisoners and staff were duly grateful'. Again, 'at no time in C and D halls did staff talk to prisoners, though when we carried out observations in E-hall we sometimes heard officers from one division giving instructions to prisoners to get up.'[26] In the evening, contact between officer and

---

[26]King and Elliott, 1977, 219.

prisoner was minimal. King and Elliott's measures of 'social distance' between uniformed staff and prisoners revealed that, overall, the amount of formal and informal contact was significantly low and far-removed from the image of benevolent interaction painted by the POA.[27] John McMillan's conclusion about relationships between prisoners and staff at Peterhead reinforced this point, and is generally valid for the prison system as a whole: 'There is a wide gulf between staff and prisoners and it is rare for staff to get close to prisoners.'[28] In 1973, an assistant governor pointed out that between prison officers and prisoners, 'no familiarity remained a normal state in prison.'[29]

The extent of the mistrust between officers and prisoners was indicated in 1971, by a report that uniformed staff were compiling a dossier for the Home Office of cases of alleged attempts to poison or injure them. It is also a significant indicator of the gulf between officers and prisoners that none of those cases was actually investigated, but was only ever suspected. It was stated, but never demonstrated, for example, that:

> Microdot tablets of LSD had been left in places where prison staff could pick them up by accident.
>   An officer told me: 'What some of them do is to place these tiny drug tablets on the landing rails where officers often lean to observe the conduct of inmates going to and from their cells. These drugs can have a devastating effect just by being absorbed through the pores of the skin.[30]

Relationships between officers and specific groups of prisoners are particularly bad. Allegations of racism among officers were fuelled by the revelations that seventy of 300 prison officers at Strangeways, Manchester, were members of the National Front. Philip Whitehead, MP, asked the Home Secretary to investigate reports of prison officers wearing National Front insignia on tiepins, and harrasing and humiliating black and Jewish prisoners.[31] In 1980, the National

---

[27]ibid., 220-21.
[28]McMillan, 1971, 2.
[29]*Guardian*, 14 September 1973.
[30]*The Times*, 23 May 1975.
[31]ibid., 24 December 1976.

Front claimed to have sympathizers and members in probably all prisons, and to be particularly strong in Walton, Pentonville, Strangeways, Wormwood Scrubs and Leeds.[32]

Not only are relationships between officers and prisoners substantially different to those outlined by the POA, but the General Secretary's claim that 'prisoners turn initially to officers' with welfare problems is not a consequence of good relationships, but of official procedures. To see welfare workers, prisoners must make an application to the landing and principal officers of their wing. Usually, they are made to divulge the nature of the problem before permission is granted.

Indeed, as the May Report acknowledged, far from wanting an involvement with welfare staff, many officers openly resent the introduction of probation officers and social workers into the prisons, identifying both the philosophy behind welfare and the welfare workers themselves as sympathetic to prisoners, and likely to line up with prisoners against them. Welfare workers are seen as concerned only with prisoners' interests and hostile to the custodial role of officers. Consequently, officers have tried to exert control over the activities of probation officers and social workers inside the prisons, by insisting (not very successfully) that welfare personnel should not carry keys, but should be dependent on uniformed staff to move them around the prison. In prison officers' recent industrial action, part-time welfare workers have been locked out of prisons, in part as an attempt to demonstrate the dependence of welfare workers on the co-operation and goodwill of prison staff.

Such criticisms are also levelled against civilian instructors and workers. The 1971 annual POA conference unanimously passed a resolution calling for limits on the employment of civilian staff. One delegate remarked:

> It is bad enough now with welfare officers and psychiatrists running around inside prisons with keys, but at least these people have something to lose if they step out of line. But you take a civilian workman: he turns up for duty and in next to no time he is running around with a bunch of keys.
>
> One of these days a man is going to sign on as a civilian workman just so that he can contact or associate with a Category

---

[32] *Daily Star,* 25 March 1980.

A man to help in an escape. Members of the staff will again be held to scorn for not seeing this obvious flaw.[33]

It is not only welfare personnel that uniformed staff are increasingly in conflict; relationships with the governor grades are also strained.

At the end of October 1978, governors warned that 'total breakdown is imminent in the prison system.'[34] Their statement was a response to the rapidly escalating disruption of the prisons by prison officers, whom governors had described to the House of Commons Expenditure Committee earlier in the year as probably presenting 'more difficulties than the prisoners'.[35] Indeed, in setting up the inquiry into the prison system, the Home Secretary had warned that 'relationships between prison officers and prison governorships are not good and this was one of the factors in the recent breakdown of industrial relations.'[36]

Indications of worsening, relationships can be found throughout the last ten years. In 1972, at Dartmoor, uniformed staff threatened to walk out if the governor did not reverse Home Office policy and punish prisoners taking part in peaceful demonstrations. In 1975, prison officers at Winchester petitioned the Home Office to replace the governor who, they claimed, was 'too soft' with prisoners. Evidence for the governor being 'too soft' was his insistence on an independent inquiry into an alleged assault on a prisoner by three officers.[37] It was only when the governor signed a nine-point set of rules, agreed with prison officers, that working relations were restored.[38] Similarly, prison officers have been engaged in a long-running battle with the governor of Dartmoor. In April 1977, for example, officers accused him of breaking local manning agreements during their 'twenty-four hour' protests which resulted in prisoners being locked in their cells for four days. Officers were demanding improvements in staff housing.[39] At the beginning of October 1978,

---

[33]*The Times*, 28 May 1971.
[34]ibid., 30 October 1978.
[35]ibid., 7 February 1978.
[36]*Guardian*, 22 November 1978.
[37]*Guardian*, 2 April 1975.
[38]*The Times*, 5 April 1975.
[39]*Guardian*, 16 April 1977.

the uniformed staff called for the governor's dismissal, after he had made public statements about the possible effects of their latest industrial action. Officers had kept prisoners locked up for nearly twenty-three hours each day for four consecutive days, and the governor was reported as saying:

> I am gravely concerned that my prisoners are being denied the facilities which should be provided as part of the overall treatment and training involved in a sentence of imprisonment.

A Home Office press officer had added that 'any governor whose prison's routine was disrupted became increasingly concerned at the lowering of the thresholds of tolerance between inmates and staff.' The chairman of the Dartmoor branch of the POA claimed that such remarks seemed calculated to cause prison unrest: 'For anyone connected with the Prison Department to make a statement like this is almost insane . . . It could even put our lives in danger.'[40]

The conflict between governors and uniformed staff is not only a consequence of poor industrial relations. It reflects also the hostility of many prison officers to 'outsiders' appointed to positions of authority with little experience of working in the prison system. In particular, officers are critical of direct entrants to the governor grades, and feel strongly that these positions should be part of the career structure of uniformed staff. Such governors are frequently believed to side with prisoners and outside professional staff against the officers, and so undermine the authority of custodial staff.

In their disputes with governor grades, uniformed staff have frequently conflicted with the executive of their own Association. At Dartmoor in 1978, for example, prison officers were acting against the advice of the National Executive Committee which argued that the Dartmoor action was 'premature'.[41] The Executive has also been accused by its members of failing to provide 'positive guidance',[42] and at the 1978 Conference was censured by its members for its handling of the Association's financial affairs.[43]

---

[40] *The Times*, 6 October 1978.
[41] *The Times*, 13 September 1978.
[42] *Prison Officers' Magazine*, Volume 68, Number 12, 444.
[43] *The Times*, 24 May 1978.

In their relationships with the central prison departments the full force of uniformed staff's sense of grievance is again visible. Although pay and conditions have been the most public source of discontent, this sense of grievance is most inflamed by the policy of handling 'troublesome' and maximum security prisoners.

In England and Wales, this conflict has centred on the policy of placing maximum security prisoners in a number of dispersal prisons, rather than concentrating them in a single fortress-type establishment. It was the Mountbatten Report which formalized the policy of concentration, although, (see page 22) such plans were already well advanced before the Report. The decisions of successive Home Secretaries to reject this policy in favour of the dispersal of maximum security prisoners recommended by the Radzinowicz Committee has always angered prison officers. In 1970, for example, the Chairman of the POA informed the annual conference:

> The policy of dispersal of Category A prisoners as recommended by the Radzinowicz Report . . . is tending to produce the same festering atmosphere which preceded the Parkhurst eruption, the tell-tale signs are all there and they can be ignored only at our peril. As all too frequently happens those who ignore the signs are not the people who ultimately are at risk.[44]

Again, in 1973, the POA General Secretary reminded members that the Association:

> remains constant in its belief that a policy of concentration, rather than one of dispersal, for dangerous prisoners provides the best long-term solution. The Mountbatten recommendation for the provision of a purpose-built prison . . . remains a valid one. It cannot be denied that those convicted of the most serious offences, particularly those involving violence, are precisely the prisoners who make determined efforts to escape. Indeed the recent escape at Gartree Prison underlines this. Until the present policy of

---

[44]*Prison Officers' Magazine,* Volume 60, Number 7, 203.

dispersal is changed, it is unlikely that the difficulties will lessen.[45]

Support for a policy of concentration is based on the belief that officers have been subjected to increasing numbers of assaults by prisoners, as a direct result of dispersal.

But experience in Scotland where concentration has long been official policy, suggests that this belief is without foundation. In contrast to England and Wales, maximum security prisoners are held together in a single institution, Peterhead. However, prison officers in Scotland are even more vociferous that their English colleagues in their claims to being 'at risk', their fears of the allegedly escalating numbers of assaults on staff, and their demands for special segregation units to deal with 'troublemakers'. In campaigning for the reopening of the cages at the end of 1978, for example, Scottish officers continually stressed the increasing dangers they faced in handling 'troublesome' prisoners, and the General Secretary of the Scottish Prison Offiers' Association, SPOA, argued repeatedly that his members were deeply worried by the growing number of attacks on them.[46] At least in Scotland, concentration has not proved the 'cure-all' which English prison officers believe it to be.

In the 1970s, neither system was operated solely on a dispersal or concentration basis but rather both systems had refined a containment policy based on the logic of control, simultaneously including the concentration and segregation of maximum-security prisoners. In England and Wales in May 1973, the Home Secretary effectively killed any remaining 'spirit' of dispersal policy by formally authorizing the increasing segregation of maximum security prisoners. Thus, at Albany, one of the dispersal prisons, 'short-termers were held in B hall, long-termers in C and D halls with the more difficult Category A and B prisoners and those serving very long sentences concentrated in D hall.'[47] It is clear that the question of how to handle maximum-security prisoners cannot be resolved by presenting concentration and dispersal as diametrically opposed alternatives, and that in both England and Wales and Scotland,

---

[45]*Prison Officers' Magazine*, January 1973.
[46]*The Times*, 16 November 1978.
[47]King and Elliott, 1977, 326-7.

whatever type of containment policy is adopted, uniform staff will continue to claim to be 'at risk', and in need of more protection – and more money.

There is no clear evidence that the number of assaults on prison staff is rising. Indeed, at least in Scotland, the suggestion is 'of a consistent rather than fluctuating or accelerating trend'.[48] Scottish Office figures for assaults on prison officers showed sixty-two assaults of which six were classified as serious in 1974, compared with sixty-three assaults, of which seven were serious in 1978 (up to 20 November).[49] As a prison officer who dissents from SPOA claims of increased assaults, has observed:

> A lot of false fear is being spread by hot-headed arguments from some people within the prison service who should know better. Prison officers are simply not being bashed about to anything like the degree or numbers quoted.[50]

The demand for more protection is directly linked to demands for improved pay. It has been argued, again by a prison officer that 'one key reason for the hysterical calls for the reopening of the Porterfield unit [the cages] at Inverness is hard bloody cash'.[51] While this has been denied by the SPOA, the Scottish Office have confirmed that overtime at Inverness is below the average for the service, and officers there 'have complained that as a result of the non-use of the cages, Porterfield is now overstaffed . . . opportunities for extra earnings, available when the cages were used, have been lost.[52]

In 1923, similar claims of being 'at risk' and demands for more protection were made after the murder of a prison officer in a juvenile institution. *A Report of the Departmental Committee appointed to Enquire into the Pay and Conditions of Service at the Prison and Borstal Institutions, etc.* not only refused the officers' pay claim but also 'set out figures to show that prison work was less dangerous than that of railwaymen, miners, quarrymen,

---

[48]*Scotsman*, 2 December 1978.
[49]*Scotsman*, 16 December 1978.
[50]*Scotsman*, 15 November 1978.
[51]ibid.
[52]*Glasgow Herald*, 10 November 1978.

Metropolitan policemen, or even factory workers.'[53] Since that Report, no officer has been murdered by a prisoner. Indeed, there have been no such murders for over 100 years in the adult prison system which would suggest that the present high anxiety about the 'dangerous offender' is exaggerated and that the 1923 Report's conclusions are still valid. This is neither to ignore nor to condone assaults on prison staff. Rather it is to try to put the present debates into perspective. Prison officers' interests are not served by such alarmism, which obscures the genuine problems they face.

The experience of the Special Unit at Barlinnie (see page 115) illustrates how these problems can be and are being worked out when officers and prisoners co-operate and support each other. By acknowledging that people are sent to prison *as* and not *for* punishment, officers at the Special Unit have been able both to move beyond the basic custodial role to which the majority of uniformed staff are presently tied, and also to examine in a different light the crisis of authority confronting them. It is by working with, rather than putting themselves against, other interests in the prison that officers in the Special Unit have successfully extended their role in a direction which both the POA and SPOA have consistently demanded, but demonstrably failed to achieve.

Prison officers' frustrations with the executives of their Associations, the prison department, and their own role has led to a division within the ranks of the uniformed staff. On the one hand, there are those who would respond to the present crisis of authority by demanding tougher and more hardline measures to control prisoners. In Scotland, such officers campaigned for the reopening of the cages, despite the incontrovertible evidence that 'incarceration in the cages makes really violent men even more intractable and violent.'[54] A prison officer, describing a private SPOA branch meeting at Barlinnie which discussed the reopening of the cages, quoted a 'mild-mannered' officer as saying, 'We had better get the cages open and we will throw food at them.'[55] In England and Wales, hardline officers have bemoaned the suspension of the use of control units, and resisted any attempts to extend their role beyond control

[53]*Prison Service Journal*, Number 7, July 1972, 9-10.
[54]*Scotsman*, 2 December 1978.
[55]ibid.

and discipline. One officer wrote:

> It has to be realized by one and all that many prisoners are
> dedicated enemies of society and when they come to prison
> every effort must be made to show them that society can hit
> back as hard at them as they try to do against society. In other
> words, they must be taught a lesson and we are the men to do
> the teaching.[56]

What this might involve was suggested by a prison officer who in
1978 was alleged to have argued that 'all these blokes understand is a
bloody good hammering.'[57]

In direct contrast are uniformed staff who have increasingly come
to realize that the present system of imprisonment damages and
degrades both prisoners and prison officers. In Scotland, it is the
officers at the Special Unit who have argued this line most
consistently and forcefully. In England and Wales, particular officers
have refused to accept any more prisoners, arguing that the facilities
to cope with them do not exist. At Ashford Remand Centre, for
example, officers drew attention to the appalling conditions on the
landings:

> On the top wings in the summer the temperature didn't drop
> below a hundred. The lads just sat, packed three to a cell in an
> atmosphere of urine. We have written to the department and
> lobbied MPs, but nobody has been concerned that these lads
> have been caged like animals. Now we have had to take the law
> into our own hands so that they can be treated humanely.[58]

The Ashford officers forced a cut-back in numbers from 450 to 260
in the space of two weeks, insisted that there should only be one
prisoner to a cell, and refused to accept more.

The National Prisoners' Movement (PROP) has shown itself to be
aware of this division within the ranks of uniformed staff, and called
for support for the 'calmer voices' among prison officers, arguing:

---

[56]*Prison Officers' Magazine,* Volume 66, Number 12, 406.
[57]*Sunday Times,* 8 October 1978.
[58]*PROP,* Volume 2, Number 6, Winter 1978/9.

There are some prison officers who, precisely because they have seen at first hand the brutalization which is inherent in the prison system are fearful of what lies ahead for prisoners and prison officers alike.[59]

Experience in Scotland, with the success of hardline uniformed staff in securing the reopening of the cages, and the increasing isolation of officers at the Special Unit, suggests that the 'calmer voices' among Britain's prison officers will be ignored.

---

[59]ibid.

6 REFORMING THE REFORMED

Throughout this book we have looked at the policies and practices of the British prison system. We have raised questions about, and frequently criticized different aspects of imprisonment. We are not alone in looking harshly at the prisons. As we have sought to show, criticism has been levelled by many different groups and individuals against either the system as a whole, or particular features of it. Thus, for example, uniformed staff have been vociferous in their condemnation of the central prison administration. An assistant governor at Wormwood Scrubs has challenged the claim that prison helps people to lead a 'good and useful life':

> When I first joined, people talked about reconviction rates; training was very much in vogue. All the talk was of the regime necessary to avoid reconviction. We know that whatever we do, it seems to make little difference. The whole process seems at best negative, at worst positively harmful.[1]

More generally, MPs, penal reform groups, criminologists and others have challenged the whole basis of imprisonment. Robert Kilroy-Silk, for example, has argued in the House of Commons:

> Imprisonment does not deter. We have a record number of people in prison and a record crime rate. Those who go to prisons are not deterred from future acts of crime by having been to prison. They may have been sentenced to four or five

---

[1] *Radio Times*, 6-12 August 1977, 10.

months or years, but the majority of them commit further offences.[2]

Such criticisms are not new, but can be found throughout the period in which imprisonment has been used as *the* major mode of punishment. During that time, various attempts have been made to relieve the crisis in the prisons. These can be categorized as attempts to reduce the prison population; attempts to relieve the crisis of conditions by building new prisons or new facilities within existing walls; attempts to change the regimes within prisons; and attempts to silence criticism of the prison system.

REDUCING THE PRISON POPULATION

Attempts to reduce the prison population have included efforts to take people out of the prisons, as well as schemes to divert people away from them. Examples of the former include the introduction of remission and parole. As we discussed in chapter 4, schemes of remission and parole were allegedly designed to reduce the length of time served by existing prisoners. But as we showed, both schemes have led to a considerable increase in the length of sentences, as well as serving to extend the apparatus of control within the prisons.

In recent years a number of schemes have been developed to divert people away from penal institutions. These 'alternatives' to prison include Community Service Orders, and Suspended Sentences. Community Service Orders (CSOs) were first used in England and Wales in 1973 (in Scotland 1977), following the recommendations of the Wootton Committee, and the implementation of the Criminal Justice Act 1972. Instead of being sent to prison, certain categories of offenders would be sentenced to work in the community in their spare time. They would be engaged in various types of jobs for between forty and 240 hours. However, even when it was introduced, 'the CSO was riddled with confusion and ambiguity.'[3] There was no agreement about which categories of offenders the scheme would include. There was confusion about why a sentence of community

---

[2]*Hansard,* 18 March 1977: Column 794.
[3]Young, 1979, 135.

service should be imposed, and how it should be administered and implemented. For these reasons, 'its initial purpose of effecting a substantial reduction of the population was blurred.'[4] Detailed studies of the impact of CSOs indicate that the scheme does not, in practice, operate as an alternative to imprisonment. The majority of people sentenced to community service would *not* have been imprisoned, but would have been dealt with by some other non-custodial punishment.[5] As Pease has concluded, CSOs divert from custody 'in only a minority of cases, albeit a very substantial minority'.[6]

Suspended sentences have also been misused: 'of all persons awarded a suspended sentence, only somewhere between forty and fifty-five per cent would, but for the new provision, have been sentenced to imprisonment for the original offence.'[7] Evidence in the May Report indicated that, as a direct consequence of the introduction of this 'alternative' to prison, the use of imprisonment actually increased.[8] The incorporation of these 'alternatives' as *additions* to the prison system highlights the interconnections between the prison, the court and the police. The limited success of such schemes as CSOs and suspended sentences indicates that a reduction of the prison population can only be achieved by effectively limiting the power of sentencers, and by radically altering police methods and targets which provide the court cases in the first instance.

RELIEVING PRISON CONDITIONS

It is frequently argued that the only way to ease the often appalling conditions inside British prisons is to build new establishments, and close down existing facilities. But there is little evidence to show that conditions are necessarily much improved in new prisons. On the contrary King and Elliott's study of Albany shows that life in the new prisons can be even more oppressive than in the Victorian relics.

---

[4]ibid.
[5]Willis, 1977, 124-5.
[6]Pease, 1980, 35.
[7]ibid.
[8]Beaumont, 1980, 13-16.

Experience at prisons such as Albany and Gartree provides support for the testimony that:

> The basic evils of imprisonment are that it denies autonomy, degrades dignity, impairs or destroys self-reliance, inculcates authoritarian values, minimizes the likelihood of beneficial interaction with one's peers, fractures family ties, destroys the family's economic stability, and prejudices the prisoner's future prospects for any improvement in his economic and social status. It does all of these things *whether* or *not* the buildings are antiseptic or dry, the aroma that of fresh bread or stale urine, the sleeping accommodation a plank or inner-sprung mattress or the interaction of inmates takes place in cells and corridors ('idleness') or in the structured setting of a particular time and place ('group therapy').[9]

As we showed in chapter 2, all the evidence suggests that prisons intended as substitutes for existing facilities become extensions to, rather than replacements for, the existing prison network, and simply provide for an ever-increasing prison population. Moreover temporary accommodation designed to meet a specific need, quickly becomes permanent. As Justin Atholl has remarked about Dartmoor, built in 1806:

> Remembering that in England nothing is so permanent as the temporary, it is fitting, if regrettable, that Dartmoor should be our most famous prison. It was erected in an emergency to meet a passing need and has survived for nearly a century and a half as the most substantial temporary structure in the world . . . If they hear statements that Dartmoor will be replaced, the ghosts that haunt the prison must laugh – or yawn, because they have heard it so often before.[10]

Atholl was writing in 1953. In 1979, the May Report recommended the closure of Dartmoor. Within hours of the Report being published, the Home Secretary had rejected the recommendation.

---

[9] American Friends Service Committee, 1971, 33.
[10] Atholl, 1953, 9.

CHANGING PRISON REGIMES

As well as attempting to change the physical fabric of the prison system, the prison authorities have sought to cope with the crisis inside by altering prison regimes. We showed in chapter 4 that such changes have most frequently and explicitly been designed to extend surveillance and control over prisoners.

Even when attempts have been made to introduce more enlightened prison policies, they have frequently been subverted by prison staff. It is clear, for instance, that opposition to the Barlinnie Special Unit, despite, or perhaps because of its unparalleled achievements, has prevented any extension of the Unit's philosophy, and even sought to undermine its continued existence (see chapter 5).

Improvements of facilities such as education and recreation have also provided increased opportunities for uniformed staff to exert greater control over the day-to-day running of the prisons, and on occasion, the opposition of staff has prevented the introduction of experimental changes in prison life. Overall, as we have already said, the commitment of uniformed staff to containment policies has proved an effective barrier not only to any extension of their role beyond that of 'custodian' or 'screw', but also to the introduction of 'more enlightened' regimes.

SILENCING THE CRITICS

Another response to the prison crisis has been the attempts by the prison authorities to silence or marginalize those people who are critical of the system. In November 1979, Jonathan Pollitzer, an official prison visitor to Wormwood Scrubs, was dismissed for publicly describing injuries to prisoners sustained after members of the MUFTI squad had broken up an apparently peaceful demonstration by prisoners. The Home Office wrote to Mr Pollitzer:

> The view which you may have formed of the incident at Wormwood Scrubs in August 31st does not of itself affect the decision to terminate the appointment. Whatever your views may have been, any evidence available to you as a prison visitor could and should have been offered to the governor or to the

official enquiry into the incident. Your insistence on broadcasting your personal comments on these matters is however, not compatible with your retention as a prison visitor.[11]

Stan Cohen and Laurie Taylor have described how they were systematically excluded from conducting academic research on the effects of long-term imprisonment, because of the earlier publication of their highly critical and widely acclaimed book *'Psychological Survival'*.[12]

There are literally hundreds of rules governing the nature of the contact between prisoners and their visitors. David Leigh has described how prisoners' friends and relatives:

> are controlled in straightforward ways – they are only allowed in with the approval of the prison administration, which can be arbitrarily limited or withdrawn; they do not have privacy for their conversation; visits may be suspended if prisoners have visible injuries after riots or disturbances, to prevent such evidence emerging; and visits may be cut short if the prisoner concerned appears to be talking out of turn. These habits are unsurprising, and well documented by civil liberties and prisoners' rights organizations. The Home Office does not seriously attempt to dispute the existence of such restrictions, which can be cloaked under a general concern for 'security'.[13]

Those who work in prisons are also subject to intensive restrictions. Both the Official Secrets Act and the prison officers' staff discipline code make it an offence to discuss publicly any aspect of the prison system. Use of the laws of libel and contempt are also effective weapons in the struggle to silence or intimidate critics.

We have discussed the extent of secrecy elsewhere (see page 6-11). The one gleam of hope in the May Report was the recognition of the need for more openness within the prison system. May recommended an inspectorate to report directly to the Home Secretary, in an

---

[11]Leigh, 1980, 113.
[12]Cohen and Taylor, 1972.
[13]Leigh, 1980, 113.

attempt to breach the walls of secrecy which shroud the prisons. 'More openness' was a phrase liberally peppered through the Report. But even May's limited proposal for an inspectorate, whose sole purpose would be advisory, without any executive function or the ability to insist on administrative or managerial change, has been resisted by a Home Office which provided the Inquiry with a series of thoroughly specious arguments against any independent review of its work.

The subversion of May's recommendations for an independent inspectorate was already well advanced before the Report was published. The Director-General of the Prison Service, in an address to a NACRO conference, originally supported the call for more openness:

> It is right that we should be under constant scrutiny. It is our job not only to act properly but also to demonstrate that we are doing so . . . we are deliberately and continuously trying to increase public understanding of the prison system, and to open that system up.[14]

But those who thought that a wind of change was blowing in the Department have since been sharply reminded of what 'more openness' means in practice. The misinformation officially handed out about the MUFTI squad's attack on D-Wing at Wormwood Scrubs in August 1979, the subsequent sacking of a prison visitor who insisted on speaking out about that attack, the apparent reluctance to appoint an internal investigation into the incident, and the fact that the MUFTI squad has been publicly congratulated on its 'professionalism' in breaking up the peaceful protest, show that the wind is still blowing in the same direction. The prison authorities appear more concerned to silence criticism than to allow independent investigation of the plethora of complaints and abuses in the British prison system.

THE CONTRADICTIONS OF IMPRISONMENT

As we have argued throughout this book, the overall impact of these

---

[14]Cited in Fitzgerald and Sim, 1980, 83.

various attempts to relieve the prison crisis has been to intensify rather than to alleviate it. In identifying and separating out different aspects of this crisis, we have sought to show how there is no single crisis but rather a series of crises deeply structured into the system of imprisonment in this country. Proposed 'reforms' of the prison system have frequently been inadequate or irrelevant to the problems facing the Service, since any proposal for change which does not reproduce existing policies and practices is defined as 'unworkable' by the prison authorities, whose own attitudes to the problems in the prison are at best ambiguous and at worst contradictory.

For example, there is a fundamental contradiction in the Home Office's explanation of why prisons exist. On the one hand it is argued that prisons exist to protect the public from dangerous people. But this argument is difficult to sustain. There certainly are people inside prisons who have been sentenced for acts which are 'dangerous to the public', but can it seriously be maintained that every one of the 50,000 people in British prisons has posed such a threat?

In England and Wales, in 1979, 32,823 adult men were sent directly to prison. Of this number 18,821 (57.3 per cent) were imprisoned for non-violent, petty property offences. A total of 111 men were imprisoned for sleeping out, and 742 for drugs offences. Of the 1,800 adult women convicted, 121 were sentenced for offences related to prostitution, fifty-six for drug offences and six for begging and sleeping out. Furthermore, 12,132 men were sent to prison for non-payment of fines, of whom 2,897 had originally been convicted of drunkenness, begging and sleeping out. Similarly 726 women were sentenced for non-payment of fines, of whom 156 were originally convicted of drunkenness and offences related to prostitution.[15]

In Scotland a similar picture emerges. In 1979, of the 5,905 men and women sent directly to prison, 3,703 (62.7 per cent) were sentenced for non-violent petty property offences. The largest category of offences for which men and women were sentenced was labelled in the Scottish Prison Department Report as 'miscellaneous'. This included thirty-one per cent of all men and women sent directly to prison during the year. It comprised offences such as breach of the

---

[15]*Prison Statistics, England and Wales*, 1979: Tables 4.1 and 5.1.

peace for which 1,059 adults were imprisoned, vagrancy for which eighty-three men were imprisoned, and prostitution, for which one woman was convicted.

In addition, 5,072 adults were imprisoned for non-payment of fines. This category constituted forty-six per cent of all those sentenced during the year. Within this group seventy-seven men had originally been convicted for vagrancy, five women for prostitution and 1,633 men and women for breach of the peace.[16] We must also remember that it is *acts* which are dangerous, and the law attaches a very particular meaning to the concept of 'dangerous'. As Mathiesen has observed:

> In our society, acts dangerous to fellow human beings are increasingly being committed. Largely, however, these acts are committed by individuals and classes with considerable power in society. Pollution, exploitation of labourers in a manner dangerous to their health, production forms which ruin the life-standard of the working class, and so on, are acts for which the most powerful members of society are in the last analysis responsible.[17]

Bottoms cites a report of the Parliamentary Commissioner for Administration on *Danger to Health from Asbestos* to illustrate this:

> [The Report] covered events at a factory at Acre Mill, Hebden Bridge, Yorkshire, until its closure in 1970. From 1954 until 1970, more than seventy deaths from asbestosis occurred among the factory's workers. Although repeated criticism was made by factory inspectors of conditions at the plant, no prosecution was ever brought.[18]

As the work of Carson and others demonstrates, this is not an isolated example. Even when prosecutions of the socially harmful activities of the powerful are successful, penalties are slight. For example, in 1978 the Ford Motor Company of Great Britain was

---

[16]*Prisons in Scotland,* 1979: Appendix 7.
[17]Mathiesen, 1974, 77-8.
[18]Bottoms, 1977, 83.

fined a total of £650 after two workmen were injured in 'accidents' at work. In the first case, in which a worker lost his right hand, the company admitted having a dangerous machine not securely fenced, and was fined £250. In the second, Ford was fined £400 after being found guilty of failing to provide a safe working system after a worker had been dragged along a conveyor belt and trapped beneath a cooling machine.[19]

That these incidents were prosecuted and reported as 'industrial accidents' rather than crimes illustrates 'the myth that crime is largely the prerogative of classes other than those which own, control and manage manufacturing industry.'[20] The Scottish Council on Crime recognized that 'in any one year, the number of persons killed on the roads in Scotland, is more than twenty times the numbers of victims of murder.'[21] As Bottoms comments:

> There is very much greater scope for the saving of lives in this area than by the preventive confinement of assaultive persons . . . we imprison for causing death by dangerous driving far less than we do for burglary, and only slightly more than we do for shoplifting. Being drunk and in charge very rarely results in imprisonment.[22]

But, on being confronted with the incontrovertible evidence that the majority of people who are imprisoned are sent for non-violent offences against property, the prison authorities shift their argument. Imprisonment exists, it is insisted, not only to protect the public but also to help people sent to prison to lead a 'good and useful life'. But, again, there is no evidence that the prison system helps people to lead a good and useful life. On the contrary, there is considerable evidence to show that imprisonment is positively harmful. Martinson, for example, analysed all the relevant research published in the English language between 1945 and 1967 (a total of 231 reports) and concluded that 'with few and isolated exceptions the rehabilitation efforts that have been reported so far had no

---

[19]*Guardian*, 28 November 1978.
[20]*Sunday Times*, 11 April 1976.
[21]Cited in Bottoms, 1977, 83.
[22]ibid.

appreciable effect on recidivism.'[23] And Shirley Summerskill, a former Minister of State at the Home Office with particular responsibility for the prisons, has argued:

> We must keep questioning the benefit of a custodial sentence. A sample of people who were given custodial sentences for serious criminal offences in January 1971 was studied by the Home Office. It was found that by the end of 1976 about seventy per cent of these people had been reconvicted. It makes a very depressing statistic.[24]

Scotland provides another depressing set of statistics. Of the 10,452 adult men sentenced to prison in Scotland in 1979, 7,009 (sixty-eight per cent) had served previous sentences of imprisonment. This included 1,615 men who had served between six and ten previous sentences; 884 who had served between eleven and twenty; and 226 who had been imprisoned twenty or more times previously.[25]

The May Report acknowledged that 'the rhetoric of treatment and training has had its day and should be replaced', proposing to replace it with 'positive custody'.[26] The Prison Department has seized on the opportunity presented by May not to change radically its present policies, but to justify existing penal practices.

As the Director-General of the Prison Services has made clear:

> I very much welcome what the Committee said about the objectives of imprisonment: None of us is starry-eyed these days about the rehabilitative value of prison. But that is no reason to give up attempts to provide constructive regimes in prisons and fall back on 'humane containment' or 'warehousing' as some have argued. Such a course offers no hope to staff who very honourably wish to make a positive contribution to the lives of their charges; equally it offers no chance to the prisoner of making the best of a bad job. The May Committee's concept of positive custody is one which not only reflects much of what

---

[23]Cited in *New Society*, 13 December 1979, 594.
[24]*Hansard*, 24 March 1980: Column 1367.
[25]*Prisons in Scotland*, 1979: Appendix 12.
[26]May Report, 1979: Paragraph 4.27.

already happens in our prisons, it also is one which points the direction in which we hope to go in the future.[27]

It is precisely these policies which are responsible for much of the present unrest, particularly in the dispersal prisons, the site of the most serious disturbances in recent years. For the May Report simply to redefine the purposes of imprisonment and to accept uncritically such policies was wholly irresponsible. In discussing the aims of imprisonment, the Report completely disregarded the achievements of the Barlinnie Special Unit. It is indeed remarkable that the Special Unit is not even mentioned in the discussion of regimes, and receives a mere two lines in a report of 347 pages.

A similar set of contradictions surrounds the introduction of 'alternatives' to imprisonment. As we have made clear in our discussion of Community Service Orders and suspended sentences, both designed to keep people out of prison, such 'alternative' schemes have succeeded only in being incorporated into the existing prison system as additions. As alternatives become additions so the overall number of people who come into contact with the prison service continues to rise. Stan Cohen has concluded:

> The major results of the new network of social control have been to increase rather than decrease the *amount* of intervention directed at many groups of offenders and to increase rather than decrease the total *number* of offenders who get into the system in the first place. In other words, 'alternatives' become not alternatives at all but new programmes which supplement the existing system or else expand the system by attracting new populations – the net of social control is widened.[28]

It is not only the *actual* impact of 'alternatives' which is problematic. The term 'community' is also loosely defined:

Community only exists for middle-class, white, healthy

---

[27] Cited in Fitzgerald and Sim, 1980, 82-3.
[28] Cohen, 1979, 20-1.

middle-aged, socially powerful males. The rest have all been classified by them.[29]

When listening to all the official talk about reducing the prison population, it is worth remembering what happened in the 1980 prison officers' dispute. During the industrial action taken by uniformed staff, the number of prisoners, and the amount of overcrowding fell sharply as staff refused to accept any new prisoners. The authorities were forced either to keep people in police or army custody, or, more interestingly, to divert people away from custody altogether. Yet as soon as the dispute was settled, instead of using the experience during the period of industrial action as an argument for a much reduced daily prison population, the Home Secretary sought a return to normal levels of imprisonment at the earliest opportunity.

Yet another contradiction is found in the relationship between prisons and the law. Offenders who defy the law are sent to prison, but the rule of law stops at the prison gates, and does not operate inside the walls. Moreover, the prison authorities have vigorously resisted any attempt to introduce the rule of law into penal institutions. Prisons remain essentially lawless. As Zellick has observed:

> Whatever attitudes one may have about crime and criminals it cannot be right that the law may be broken with impunity. That is why we sent people to prison in the first place. What kind of experience is imprisonment likely to be if those set in authority over prisoners express a contempt for the law and its processes different only in degree from the offences committed by those in their charge?[30]

The denial of access to the law has severe consequences for the imprisoned:

> Normal legal principles applying to every other public institution deriving its authority from the state do not apply to

---

[29]ibid., 25.
[30]Graham Zellick, cited in *The Times*, 9 August 1977.

prisons. Any violation of the Prison Act or Rules by the authorities, no matter how much damage this causes a prisoner is not actionable.[31]

It is not surprising that a concerted challenge to the lawlessness of prisons is presently being launched. It was given its impetus in 1975, when the European Court of Human Rights in Strasbourg found in favour of a prisoner, Sydney Golder, who had been refused permission to contact directly a solicitor about possible libel action against a prison officer:

> Golder claimed that the Home Office had violated Articles 6 and 8 of the European Convention of Human Rights. According to Article 6, 'Everyone is entitled to a fair and public hearing within a reasonable time by an independent and impartial tribunal established by law.' As Golder was not even allowed to see a lawyer how could he exercise such a right? Despite some legal chop-logic from government lawyers who claimed that the right to a fair trial did not include the actual right to have a trial, the court found for Golder. They also ruled that Prison Rule 34(8) which had prevented him from writing directly to a solicitor was a violation of Article 8 of the Convention which lays down that a public authority should not interfere with an individual's right to respect for his correspondence.[32]

But as Anthony Trollope has noted, the Home Office promptly subverted this ruling:

> In response to this decision (the Golder Case) the Home Office introduced a new Rule 37A which was intended to appear to remove the objectionable features of Rule 34(8) but in fact has done little or nothing of the kind and the situation remains in fact nearly as it did before. Firstly a prisoner can write to his lawyer about legal proceedings with which he is actually involved such as a criminal charge he is facing. Secondly he may

---

[31]Cohen and Taylor, 1977, 24.
[32]Taylor, 1978, 172.

write to a solicitor for legal advice in connection with any civil proceedings to which he may become a party or which he wishes to take, subject to any directions of the Home Secretary.

The result is that unless a prisoner wants advice about a civil case he is likely to be involved in Rule 37A does not help him. It does not cover criminal proceedings which may involve him in the future nor may a prisoner obtain advice where no proceedings are in the offing.[33]

In another court decision in October 1978, prisoners in England and Wales were given the right to appeal to outside courts or agencies against verdicts handed out in disciplinary hearings by boards of visitors. This decision followed from the Hull riot in August 1976 (see page 9), when a prisoner applied for *certiorari* alleging that the Board of Visitors' hearing after the riot had not been carried out in accordance with the principles of natural justice. While the Divisional Court unanimously refused the application, the Court of Appeal reversed the Divisional Court's decision. In his summing up in the Appeal Court, Lord Justice Shaw pointed out that the courts are in general the ultimate custodians of the rights and liberties of the subject whatever his or her status and however attenuated these rights and liberties may be as the result of some punitive or other process.[34] While it has been recognized that this decision was 'a step in the right direction', in moving towards granting prisoners the same legal rights as anyone else there is still a long way to go.

While prisoners in England and Wales now have the right to appeal against the sentences of Boards of Visitors to an outside court, the procedures and charges they face in disciplinary proceedings remain intact. (Scottish prisoners are not covered by the judgement). The contradiction remains: people sent to prison for being law-breakers are held in lawless places.

The 'place' of the prison system is similarly contradictory. On the one hand, prisoners are separated out, isolated from the rest of the community. The high walls, strict surveillance, barbed wire, myriad of rules and restrictions regulating access to the prisons, and the secrecy which surrounds them serve not only to keep prisoners in, but

---

[33]*Guardian*, 17 November 1980.
[34]Cited in Tettenborn, 1980, 88.

everyone else out. The separation of the prison serves as an important social metaphor, a clear dividing line between 'good' and 'evil', a grim warning to would-be law-breakers. As an encyclopaedia article on prison architecture, written in 1826 made clear, prison buildings offer:

> an effectual method of exciting the imagination to a most desirable point of abhorrence. Persons, in general, refer their horror of prisons to an instinctive feeling rather than to any accurate knowledge of the privations or inflictions therein endured . . . The exterior of a prison should, therefore, be formed in the heavy and sombre style which most frequently impresses the spectator with gloom and terror.[35]

At the same time, prisons are an integral part of the criminal justice system. It is the courts who send people to prison, the police who take people to court. We have already noted that any attempt to reduce the imprisoned population must be directed at the courts and the police – and not at the prisons.

Even this relationship is problematic. A rising crime rate is taken to be threatening to social order and indicative of a more general social malaise. But a rising prison rate is seen as a sign of success in the struggle to uphold social order. As Merlyn Rees, former Labour Home Secretary, remarked: 'one sign of success in the fight for law and order is that more people are in prison.'

As Rees' remark suggests, the prison system is interconnected with the creation and maintenance of social order. We saw, for example, how prisons provide a particular definition of 'dangerousness', a specific image of 'crime' and 'the criminal' (page 154). Indeed, the *character* of imprisonment is derived directly from wider social order. The relationships between class, law, crime and crime control have been analysed extensively in much recent criminological work.[36] Specific links between social order and imprisonment have been explored most fully in the recent revisionist history of the prison system.

---

[35]Cited in Johnston, 1973, 26-7.
[36]For a summary of this work see Hall and Scraton, 1981.

REFORMING THE REFORMED

The importance of the work of Foucault, Rothman and Ignatieff has been to convert the narrow institutional history of imprisonment into a social history of the philosophy and practice of power and authority in general. The prison is no longer analysed as an isolated object of study in and of itself, but rather as a focus for the mapping of much broader changes in class relations, power and authority.

The accounts of the history of the prison system enable us to identify the contradictions of imprisonment and locate historically the crises in the prison. Ignatieff, for example, has shown how the new model prisons of the early nineteenth century substituted the 'pains of intention' for the 'pains of neglect'.[37] Thus regular diets replaced fitful, occasionally non-existent provision of food in eighteenth century institutions; uniforms replaced rags and personal clothing; prisoners received regular medical attention. A new range of hygienic rituals, including head-shaving, medical examination and bathing on reception, and regular cleaning of the prison and its occupants, were introduced. But with the new hygiene came a new figure in the penal landscape: the prison doctor. From the beginning the doctors' role was contradictory. On the one hand, they were responsible for the health and well-being of individuals. On the other, they were deeply implicated in the health and well-being of the institution

As a result of this historical work, we can also identify the origins of the concern with containment and security. Prior to their reform in the early nineteenth century, prisons had been based on the 'rule of custom'. Accounts of eighteenth century prisons highlight the 'autonomy' and 'self-government' of prisoners within the walls. Prisoners awaiting trial, and debtors were not subjected to any coercive routine, and often ran the prisons themselves, allocating cells, establishing their own rules, grievance procedures and system of punishments. Ignatieff also shows how it was common for wives to appear daily at the gates with meals for jailed husbands, and for prisoners to be given 'the run of prison yards from dawn until locking up, and a judiciously placed bribe would make it possible to remain

---

[37]Ignatieff, 1978, 100-13.

at night.'[38] There was then an 'easy commerce' between the prison and the streets.

It was precisely these arrangements to which reformers such as John Howard, objected. They sought to end prisoners' relatively easy access to their families and friends, and to the world outside the institution.

In the reformed prisons, the social distance between the prison and the outside world was firmly established. Access was limited and regularized. Within the prisons, prisoners were categorized, separated out from each other, and subjected to a series of new internal rules aimed at preventing or regulating communications between them. Central to these new regimes were the principles of inspection and surveillance. The architecture of the proposed 'model' prisons incorporated the principles and philosophies of the new regimes. Bentham's Panopticon, for example, was designed to facilitate the maximum observation of prisoners by guards and to ensure that prisoners, whether or not they were actually being observed, should feel that they were. Thus:

> A plan was devised in which no part of the prison would be free from the potential observation of an inspector and in which the inspector's view of prisoners would be optimized. The prison was to be circular or polygonal. The cells were to be placed around the inside of the circumference; in the centre of the circle was to be placed the inspection-house, in which the inspector or guard was to be situated. From the inspection house the cells were to be visible. The front of the cells were to be secured through an iron grid which would allow for total visibility of the inside of the cell by the inspector.[39]

In this way, the new prisons provided the structural basis of the new regimes. By replacing the 'rule of custom' with the 'rule of rules', the seeds of the obsession with containment and control had been planted.

In the same way, the enforcement of a markedly greater social distance between the imprisoned and the outside world severely

---

[38]ibid., 34.
[39]Fine, 1974, 1.

curtailed the visibility of the prisons, and eroded the opportunities for visitors to check on the activities of the guards. Prisoners became increasingly vulnerable to the abuses of authority, and with the eventual centralization of the prison system and the imposition of official secrecy, the possibility of any independent scrutiny of the prison authorities and their activities disappeared.

In this way, revisionist history has alerted us to the contradictory nature of reform. Thomas Mathiesen, in arguing for radical change in the prison system has sought to distinguish between 'positive' and 'negative' reforms.[40] Positive reforms, he argues are those which strengthen the prison system, whereas negative reforms chip away at, rather than facilitate the expansion of the system. But no such distinction can be made. Reform, *by its very nature*, contains both positive and negative possibilities. Thus, the hygienic rituals advocated by the early prison reformers, a 'negative' reform in that they ended 'gaol fever' which caused the death of so many prisoners and staff, were also a positive reform, a means of regimenting and humiliating the imprisoned:

> On entry, convicts . . . were stripped naked, probed and examined by a doctor and then bathed, shaved and uniformed. This purification rite cleansed them of vermin and filth, but it also stripped them of those marks of identity that defined them as persons. Offenders' individualities were recast in the ghostly sameness of cropped hair and institutional clothing. Latently, the admission ritual brought home to offenders the state's power to subject every outward feature of their identity to control. Similarly, the daily clean-ups and hygienic inspections were intended not only to guard against disease, but also to express the state's power to order every feature of the institutional environment, no matter how minor.[41]

In proposing changes to the prison system, then, we must always be aware of the contradictory nature of reform, and struggle to ensure that changes which do occur do not covertly extend the

---

[40]Mathiesen, 1974.
[41]Ignatieff, 1978, 101.

massive apparatus of repressive control which is the hallmark of the contemporary British prison system.

The revisionist history has alerted us to the historical derivation of the present prison crisis and provides an explanation for it. But much work remains to be done. As Ignatieff has acknowledged:

> We are still awaiting a new historiography of the disintegration of the nineteenth century penitentiary routines, of lock-step and silence; the rise of probation, parole and juvenile court; the ascendency of the psychiatric and social work professions within the carceral system; the history of drug use as therapeutic and control devices; the impact of electronic and TV surveillance systems on the nineteenth century institutional inheritance; the unionization of custodial personnel; the impact of rising standards of living upon levels of institutional amenity and inmate expectation; the long-term pattern of sentencing and the changing styles of administrative and judicial discretion; the history of ethnic and race relations within the walls; the social and institutional origins of the waves of prison rioting in the 1950s and late 1960s.[42]

But the most salutary lesson of revisionist history is that the contemporary prison system is *the reformed prison system*. The crisis in the prisons then is the crisis of reform, the seeds of which were sown when the prisons were reconstituted in the early nineteenth century as part of a wider struggle to impose new forms of class domination.

In arguing and working for change in the prisons we must continually remind ourselves of the direct links between the prison and that wider struggle. Although the prison has often been characterized as a 'closed world' many of its features which we struggle against are specific forms of a more general phenomenon being developed in the wider social system. For example, the 'logic of containment' discussed in chapter 4 can be found outside the prison walls. The creation and management of 'troublemakers' in prisons is paralleled by the increasing medicalization of the definition and control of 'problem children' in school. In both institutions, there

---

[42] Ignatieff, 1981.

has been a rapid acceleration in the use of segregation. The number of special units in schools to deal with the 'disruptive behaviour' of particular children rose from forty in 1973 to 239 in 1978.[43]

Containment policies in prison, then, are not simply organizational or bureaucratic responses to the problem of holding an increasing number of people serving long sentences. They are part of a more general response to a crisis of control which exists beyond the prison walls.

In making the connections between the prison and the outside world, we are signalling general questions about the nature of social order and state authority. In this increasingly intolerant and punitive society, we must to challenge not only the nature and extent but also the continuing existence of imprisonment. And as the demands for law and order become more strident we should always remember that:

> The ultimate expression of law is not order – it's prison. We have hundreds of prisons, and thousands upon thousands of laws, yet there is no social order, no social peace.[44]

---

[43] *Guardian*, 24 January 1979.
[44] Jackson, 1972, 119.

SELECT BIBLIOGRAPHY

Absalom, J. 1970: 'The Prison Officer', *The Criminologist*, November.

American Friends Service Committee, 1971: *Struggle for Justice: A Report on Crime and Punishment in America*, Hill and Wang.

Atholl, J. 1953: *Prison on the Moor*, John Long.

Beaumont, B. 1980: 'Reducing the Prison Population – A Political Choice', *Probe*, May.

Bottomley, A. Keith, 1973: *Decisions in the Penal Process*, Martin Robertson.

Bottoms, A. E. 1977: 'Reflections on the Renaissance of Dangerousness', *The Howard Journal*, Volume XVI, Number 2.

Boyle, J. 1977: *A Sense of Freedom*, Pan Books.

Briggs, D. 1975: *In Place of Prison*, Temple-Smith, New Society.

Caird, R. 1974: *A Good and Useful Life*, Hart-Davis, MacGibbon.

Cohen, S. 1977: 'Prisons and the Future Control of Systems: From Concentration to Dispersal', in Fitzgerald, M., Halmos, P., Muncie, J., and Zeldin, D., editors, *Welfare in Action*, Routledge and Kegan Paul/The Open University Press.

Cohen, S. 1979: *Crime and Punishment: Some Thoughts on Theories and Policies*, Radical Alternatives to Prison.

Cohen, S. and Taylor, L. 1972: *Psychological Survival: The Experience of Long-Term Imprisonment*, Penguin Books.

Cohen, S. and Taylor, L. 1977: 'Talkin' Prison Blues' in Bell, C. and Newby, H., editors, *Doing Sociological Research*, Allen and Unwin.

Cohen, S. and Taylor, L. 1978: *Prison Secrets*, National Council for Civil Liberties/Radical Alternatives to Prison.

Colvin, E. 1978: 'Prison Officers: A Sociological Portrait of the

168   *Select Bibliography*

Uniformed Staff of an English Prison', unpublished Ph.D. thesis, University of Cambridge.

Cronin, H. 1967: *The Screw Turns,* John Long.

Cross, R., 1971: *Punishment, Prison and the Public,* Stevens.

Evans, P. 1980: *Prison Crisis,* Allen and Unwin.

Fine B. 1974: 'Objectification and the Contradictions of Bourgeois Power: Sartre and the Modern Prison', unpublished version of revised paper in *Economy and Society,* Volume 6, Number 4.

Fitzgerald, M. 1977: *Prisoners in Revolt,* Penguin Books.

Fitzgerald, M. and Sim, J. 1980: 'Legitimating the Prison Crisis: A Critical Review of the May Report', *The Howard Journal,* Volume XIX.

Foucault, M. 1977: *Discipline and Punish: The Birth of the Prison,* Allen Lane.

Hall, S. and Scraton, P., 1981: 'Law, Class and Control', in Fitzgerald, M., McLennon, G. and Pawson, J., compilers, *Issues in Crime and Society,* Routledge and Kegan Paul.

Home Office, Scottish Home and Health Department and Northern Ireland Office, 1979: *Evidence Submitted to the Inquiry into the United Kingdom Prison Services* (3 volumes), HMSO.

Ignatieff, M. 1978: *A Just Measure of Pain,* MacMillan.

Ignatieff, M. 1981: 'State, Civil Society and Total Institutions: A Critique of Recent Sociological Theories of Punishment', *Crime and Society,* 6.

Jackson, G. 1972: *Blood in My Eye,* Penguin Books.

Johnston, N. 1973: *The Human Cage: A Brief History of Prison Architecture,* New York, Walker.

Jones, H. and Cornes, P. 1977: *Open Prisons,* Routledge and Kegan Paul.

King, R. D. and Elliott, K. W. 1977: *Albany: Birth of a Prison – End of an Era,* Routledge and Kegan Paul.

King, R. D. and Morgan, R. 1976: *A Taste of Prison: Custodial Conditions for Trial and Remand Prisoners,* Routledge and Kegan Paul.

King, R. D. and Morgan, R. 1980: *The Future of the Prison System,* Gower.

Leigh, D. 1980: *The Frontiers of Secrecy,* Junction Books.

Logan, A. D. W. 1976: 'Treatment of Irish Prisoners Convicted of Terrorist Offences', *Law Society Gazette,* Volume 173.

MacDonald, D. and Sim, J. 1978: *Scottish Prisons and the Special Unit*, The Scottish Council for Civil Liberties.

McMillan, J. 1971: 'Some Notes and Observations on the Prison Subculture', unpublished.

Mathiesen, T. 1974: *The Politics of Abolition*, Martin Robertson.

May Report, 1979: *Report of the Committee of Inquiry into the United Kingdom Prison Service*, Cmnd. 76 73.

Miller, A. 1976: *Inside Out: The Story of a Prison Governor*, Queensgate Press.

Pease, K. 1980: 'Community Service and Prison: Are they Alternatives?' in Pease, K., and McWilliams, W., editors, *Community Service By Order*, Scottish Academic Press.

Playfair, G. 1971: *The Punitive Obsession*, Gollancz.

Prewer, R. R. 1974: 'The Contribution of Prison Medicine', in Blom-Cooper, L., editor, *Progress in Penal Reform*, Oxford University Press.

Probyn, W. 1977: *Angel Face : The Making of a Criminal*, Allen and Unwin.

PROP, 1977: *Hull 1976*, PROP, London.

Release, 1978: *Trouble with the Law*, Pluto Press.

Ruggles-Brise, Sir E. 1921: *The English Prison System*, Macmillan.

Schwendinger, H. and Schwendinger, J. (undated) 'Standards of Life in Penal Institutions', unpublished.

Scottish Information Office Reference Unit, 1978: *Prisons and other Penal Establishments in Scotland*.

Smart, C. 1977: *Woman, Crime and Criminology*, Routledge and Kegan Paul.

Sparks, R. F. 1971: *Local Prisons: The Crisis in the English Penal System*, Heinemann.

Taylor, L. 1978: 'Onslaught on Prison Secrecy', *New Statesman*, 11 August.

Tettenborn, A. 1980: 'Prisoners Rights', *Public Law*.

Thomas, J. E. 1972: *The English Prison Officer Since 1850: A Study in Conflict*, Routledge and Kegan Paul.

Walker, H. 1980: 'Alternatives to Imprisonment', *Probation Journal*, Volume 27, Number 2.

Webb, S. and Webb, B. 1963: *English Prisons under Local Government*, Frank Cass.

Willis, A. 1977: 'Community Service as an Alternative to

Imprisonment: A Cautionary View', *Probation Journal*, Volume 24, Number 4.

Young, W. 1979: *Community Service Orders*, Heinemann.

The National Prisoners' Movement (PROP) publishes a bi-monthly newspaper *PROP* available from: 97 Caledonian Road, London, N1; or 50 Westbourne Avenue, Hull.

Radical Alternatives to Prison publishes *The Abolitionist,* available from: 97 Caledonian Road, London, N1.

Both organizations provide regular information about the discussions of the prison system.

INDEX

Foucault.